Editor

Cristina Krysinski, M. Ed.

Editor in Chief

Karen J. Goldfluss, M.S. Ed.

Creative Director

Sarah M. Fournier

Cover Artist

Barbara Lorseyedi

Art Coordinator

Renée Mc Elwee

Imaging

Amanda R. Harter

Publisher

Mary D. Smith, M.S. Ed.

TCR 8247

Compr...

Using Literal, Inf... & Applied Questioning

Twenty texts presented in a variety of genres with activities to reinforce close reading

Related comprehension strategies activities for each unit

Three levels of questioning to improve comprehension and critical-thinking skills

★ Correlated to the Common Core State Standards

Teacher Created Resources

CORRELATED TO COMMON CORE STANDARDS

For correlations to the Common Core State Standards, see page 109 of this book or visit *http://www.teachercreated.com/standards*.

Teacher Created Resources

6421 Industry Way
Westminster, CA 92683
www.teachercreated.com

ISBN: 978-1-4206-8247-2

© *2015 Teacher Created Resources*
Made in U.S.A.

Teacher Created Resources

Table of Contents

Introduction

Twenty different texts from a variety of genres are included in this reading comprehension resource. These may include humor, fantasy, myth/legend, folktale, mystery, adventure, suspense, fairy tale, play, fable, science fiction, poetry, and informational/nonfiction texts, such as a timetable, letter, report, procedure, poster, map, program, book cover, and cartoon.

Three levels of questions are used to indicate the reader's comprehension of each text.

One or more particular comprehension strategies have been chosen for practice with each text.

Each unit is five pages long and consists of the following resources and strategies:

- teacher information: includes the answer key and extension suggestions
- text page: text is presented on one full page
- activity page 1:   covers literal and inferential questions
- activity page 2:   covers applied questions
- applying strategies: focuses on a chosen comprehension strategy/strategies

Teacher Information

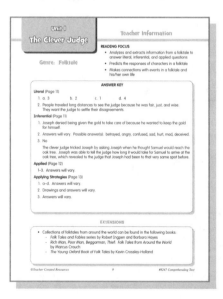

- **Reading Focus** states the comprehension skill emphasis for the unit.
- **Genre** is clearly indicated.
- **Answer Key** is provided. For certain questions, answers will vary, but suggested answers are given.
- **Extension Activities** suggest other authors or book titles. Other literacy activities relating to the text are suggested.

Text Page

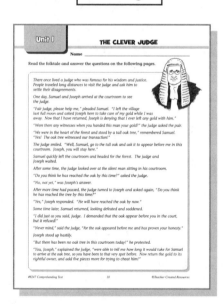

- The title of the text is provided.
- Statement is included in regard to the genre.
- Text is presented on a full page.

Activity Page 1

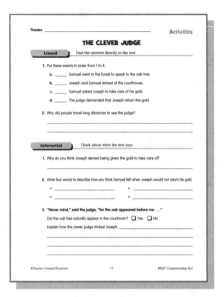

Activity Page 2

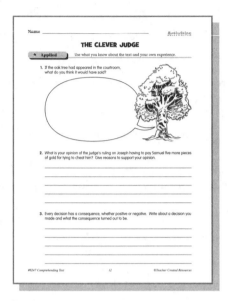

- **Literal** questions provide opportunities to practice locating answers in the text.

- **Inferential** questions provide opportunities to practice finding evidence in the text.

- **Applied** questions provide opportunities to practice applying prior knowledge.

Applying Strategies

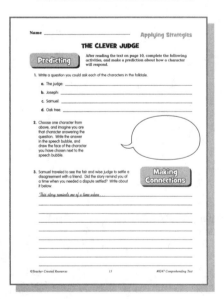

- Comprehension strategy focus is clearly labeled.

- Activities provide opportunities to utilize the particular strategy.

Types of Questions

Students are given **three types of questions** (all grouped accordingly) to assess their comprehension of a particular text in each genre:

- **Literal questions** are questions for which answers can be found directly in the text.
- **Inferential questions** are questions for which answers are implied in the text and require the reader to think a bit more deeply about what he or she has just read.
- **Applied questions** are questions that require the reader to think even further about the text and incorporate personal experiences and knowledge to answer them.

Answers for literal questions are always given and may be found on the Teacher Information pages. Answers for inferential questions are given when appropriate. Applied questions are best checked by the teacher following, or in conjunction with, a class discussion.

Comprehension Strategies

Several specific comprehension strategies have been selected for practice in this book.

Although specific examples have been selected, often other strategies, such as scanning, are used in conjunction with those indicated, even though they may not be stated. Rarely does a reader use only a single strategy to comprehend a text.

Strategy Definitions

Predicting
Prediction involves the students using illustrations, text, or background knowledge to help them construct meaning. Students might predict what texts could be about, what could happen, or how characters could act or react. Prediction may occur before, during, and after reading, and it can be adjusted during reading.

Making Connections
Students comprehend texts by linking their prior knowledge with the new information from the text. Students may make connections between the text and themselves, between the new text and other texts previously read, and between the text and real-world experiences.

Comparing
This strategy is closely linked to the strategy of making connections. Students make comparisons by thinking more specifically about the similarities and differences between the connections being made.

Sensory Imaging
Sensory imaging involves students utilizing all five senses to create mental images of passages in the text. Students also use their personal experiences to create these images. The images may help students make predictions, form conclusions, interpret information, and remember details.

Strategy Definitions *(cont.)*

Determining Importance/ Identifying Main Idea(s)

The strategy of determining importance is particularly helpful when students try to comprehend informational texts. It involves students determining the important theme or main idea of particular paragraphs or passages.

As students become effective readers, they will constantly ask themselves what is most important in a phrase, sentence, paragraph, chapter, or whole text. To determine importance, students will need to use a variety of information, such as the purpose for reading, their knowledge of the topic, background experiences and beliefs, and understanding of the text format.

Skimming

Skimming is the strategy of looking quickly through texts to gain a general impression or overview of the content. Readers often use this strategy to quickly assess whether a text, or part of it, will meet their purpose. Because this book deals predominantly with comprehension after reading, skimming has not been included as one of the major strategies.

Scanning

Scanning is the strategy of quickly locating specific details, such as dates, places, or names, or those parts of the text that support a particular point of view. Scanning is often used, but not specifically mentioned, when used in conjunction with other strategies.

Synthesizing/Sequencing

Synthesizing is the strategy that enables students to collate a range of information in relation to the text. Students recall information, order details, and piece information together to make sense of the text. Synthesizing/sequencing helps students to monitor their understanding. Synthesizing involves connecting, comparing, determining importance, posing questions, and creating images.

Summarizing/Paraphrasing

Summarizing involves the processes of recording key ideas, main points, or the most important information from a text. Summarizing or paraphrasing reduces a larger piece of text to the most important details.

Genre Definitions

Fiction and Poetry

Science Fiction These stories include backgrounds or plots based upon possible technology or inventions, experimental medicine, life in the future, environments drastically changed, alien races, space travel, genetic engineering, dimensional portals, or changed scientific principles. Science fiction encourages readers to suspend some of their disbelief and examine alternate possibilities.

Suspense Stories of suspense aim to make the reader feel fear, disgust, or uncertainty. Many suspense stories have become classics. These include *Frankenstein* by Mary Shelley, *Dracula* by Bram Stoker, and *Dr. Jekyll and Mr. Hyde* by Robert Louis Stevenson.

Mystery Stories from this genre focus on the solving of a mystery. Plots of mysteries often revolve around a crime. The hero must solve the mystery, overcoming unknown forces or enemies. Stories about detectives, police, private investigators, amateur sleuths, spies, thrillers, and courtroom dramas usually fall into this genre.

Fable A fable is a short story that states a moral. Fables often use talking animals or animated objects as the main characters. The interaction of the animals or animated objects reveals general truths about human nature.

Fairy Tale These tales are usually about elves, dragons, goblins, fairies, or magical beings and are often set in the distant past. Fairy tales usually begin with the phrase "Once upon a time . . ." and end with the words ". . . and they lived happily ever after." Charms, disguises, and talking animals may also appear in fairy tales.

Fantasy A fantasy may be any text or story removed from reality. Stories may be set in nonexistent worlds, such as an elf kingdom, on another planet, or in alternate versions of the known world. The characters may not be human (dragons, trolls, etc.) or may be humans who interact with non-human characters.

Folktale Stories that have been passed from one generation to the next by word of mouth rather than by written form are folktales. Folktales may include sayings, superstitions, social rituals, legends, or lore about the weather, animals, or plants.

Play Plays are specific pieces of drama, usually enacted on a stage by actors dressed in makeup and appropriate costumes.

Adventure Exciting events and actions feature in these stories. Character development, themes, or symbolism are not as important as the actions or events in an adventure story.

Humor Humor involves characters or events that promote laughter, pleasure, or humor in the reader.

Genre Definitions (cont.)

Fiction and Poetry (cont.)

Poetry
This genre utilizes rhythmic patterns of language. The patterns include meter (high- and low-stressed syllables), syllabication (the number of syllables in each line), rhyme, alliteration, or a combination of these. Poems often use figurative language.

Myth
A myth explains a belief, practice, or natural phenomenon and usually involves gods, demons, or supernatural beings. A myth does not necessarily have a basis in fact or a natural explanation.

Legend
Legends are told as though the events were actual historical events. Legends may or may not be based on an elaborated version of a historical event. Legends are usually about human beings, although gods may intervene in some way throughout the story.

Nonfiction

Letter
These are written conversations sent from one person to another. Letters usually begin with a greeting, contain the information to be related, and conclude with a farewell signed by the sender.

Report
Reports are written documents describing the findings of an individual or group. They may take the form of a newspaper report, sports report, or police report, or a report about an animal, person, or object.

Biography
A biography is an account of a person's life written by another person. The biography may be about the life of a celebrity or a historical figure.

Journal
A journal is a continued series of texts written by a person about his/her life experiences and events. Journals may include descriptions of daily events as well as thoughts and emotions.

Review
A review is a concise summary or critical evaluation of a text, event, object, or phenomenon. A review may present a perspective, argument, or purpose. It offers critical assessment of content, effectiveness, noteworthy features, and often ends with a suggestion of audience appreciation.

Other **informational texts**, such as **timetables**, are excellent sources to teach and assess comprehension skills. Others may include **diagrams**, **graphs**, **advertisements**, **maps**, **plans**, **tables**, **charts**, **lists**, **posters**, and **programs**.

Genre: Folktale

READING FOCUS

- Analyzes and extracts information from a folktale to answer literal, inferential, and applied questions
- Predicts the responses of characters in a folktale
- Makes connections with events in a folktale and his/her own life

ANSWER KEY

Literal (Page 11)

1. a. 3   b. 2   c. 1   d. 4

2. People traveled long distances to see the judge because he was fair, just, and wise. They want the judge to settle their disagreements.

Inferential (Page 11)

1. Joseph denied being given the gold to take care of because he wanted to keep the gold for himself.

2. Answers will vary. Possible answer(s): betrayed, angry, confused, sad, hurt, mad, deceived.

3. No

   The clever judge tricked Joseph by asking him when he thought Samuel would reach the oak tree. Joseph was able to tell the judge how long it would take for Samuel to arrive at the oak tree, which revealed to the judge that Joseph had been to that very same spot before.

Applied (Page 12)

1–3. Answers will vary.

Applying Strategies (Page 13)

1. a–d. Answers will vary.

2. Drawings and answers will vary.

3. Answers will vary.

EXTENSIONS

- Collections of folktales from around the world can be found in the following books:
  - *Folk Tales and Fables* series by Robert Ingpen and Barbara Hayes
  - *Rich Man, Poor Man, Beggarman, Thief: Folk Tales from Around the World* by Marcus Crouch
  - *The Young Oxford Book of Folk Tales* by Kevin Crossley-Holland

Name _____

Read the folktale and answer the questions on the following pages.

There once lived a judge who was famous for his wisdom and justice. People traveled long distances to visit the judge and ask him to settle their disagreements.

One day, Samuel and Joseph arrived at the courtroom to see the judge.

"Fair judge, please help me," pleaded Samuel. "I left the village last full moon and asked Joseph here to take care of my gold while I was away. Now that I have returned, Joseph is denying that I ever left any gold with him."

"Were there any witnesses when you handed this man your gold?" the judge asked the pair.

"We were in the heart of the forest and stood by a tall oak tree," remembered Samuel. "Yes! The oak tree witnessed our transaction!"

The judge smiled. "Well, Samuel, go to the tall oak and ask it to appear before me in this courtroom. Joseph, you will stay here."

Samuel quickly left the courtroom and headed for the forest. The judge and Joseph waited.

After some time, the judge looked over at the silent man sitting in his courtroom.

"Do you think he has reached the oak by this time?" asked the judge.

"No, not yet," was Joseph's answer.

After more time had passed, the judge turned to Joseph and asked again, "Do you think he has reached the tree by this time?"

"Yes," Joseph responded. "He will have reached the oak by now."

Some time later, Samuel returned, looking defeated and saddened.

"I did just as you said, judge. I demanded that the oak appear before you in the court, but it refused!"

"Never mind," said the judge, "for the oak appeared before me and has proven your honesty."

Joseph stood up hastily.

"But there has been no oak tree in this courtroom today!" he protested.

"You, Joseph," explained the judge, "were able to tell me how long it would take for Samuel to arrive at the oak tree, so you have been to that very spot before. Now return the gold to its rightful owner, and add five pieces more for trying to cheat him!"

THE CLEVER JUDGE

| **Literal** | Find the answers directly in the text. |

1. Put these events in order from 1 to 4.

   a. _____ Samuel went to the forest to speak to the oak tree.

   b. _____ Joseph and Samuel arrived at the courthouse.

   c. _____ Samuel asked Joseph to take care of his gold.

   d. _____ The judge demanded that Joseph return the gold.

2. Why did people travel long distances to see the judge?

   _____

   _____

| **Inferential** | Think about what the text says. |

1. Why do you think Joseph denied being given the gold to take care of?

   _____

2. Write four words to describe how you think Samuel felt when Joseph would not return his gold.

   - _____   - _____

   - _____   - _____

3. "Never mind," said the judge, "for the oak appeared before me . . ."

   Did the oak tree actually appear in the courtroom?   ☐ Yes   ☐ No

   Explain how the clever judge tricked Joseph. _____

   _____

   _____

   _____

THE CLEVER JUDGE

Applied   Use what you know about the text and your own experience.

1. If the oak tree had appeared in the courtroom,
   what do you think it would have said?

2. What is your opinion of the judge's ruling on Joseph having to pay Samuel five more pieces
   of gold for trying to cheat him? Give reasons to support your opinion.

   _____

   _____

   _____

   _____

   _____

3. Every decision has a consequence, whether positive or negative. Write about a decision you
   made and what the consequence turned out to be.

   _____

   _____

   _____

   _____

   _____

THE CLEVER JUDGE

Predicting

After reading the text on page 10, complete the following activities, and make a prediction about how a character will respond.

1. Write a question you could ask each of the characters in the folktale.

   a. The judge: _____

   b. Joseph: _____

   c. Samuel: _____

   d. Oak tree: _____

2. Choose one character from above, and imagine you are that character answering the question. Write the answer in the speech bubble, and draw the face of the character you have chosen next to the speech bubble.

Making Connections

3. In order to settle a disagreement with a friend, Samuel traveled to see the fair and wise judge. Did the story remind you of a time when you needed a dispute settled? Write about it below.

   This story reminds me of a time when . . . _____

   _____

   _____

   _____

   _____

   _____

   _____

   _____

Genre: Television Program

READING FOCUS

- Analyzes and extracts information from an informational text to answer literal, inferential, and applied questions
- Predicts what television shows will be about
- Summarizes information from an informational text

ANSWER KEY

Literal (Page 16)

1. a. Yes   b. No   c. No   d. Yes   e. Yes   f. No

2. 12:00 and 6:00

Inferential (Page 16)

1. Answers may include any of the shows from 6:00 onwards.

2. Two of the following: *A Present for Lilly, The Adventures of Thomas Crumb, Cartoon Corner, Life in the Wild, Sporting Heroes, Super Sleuth Sam.*

3. Answers will vary. Possible answer(s): many adults may be at home at this time and are able to watch them while children are in school.

Applied (Page 17)

1–3. Answers will vary.

Applying Strategies (Page 18)

1. Answers will vary.

2.

Name/Type	Number of times aired on weekdays	Suitable audience	Length of show
Daytime movies	5	Family	2 hours
Cops on the Beat	2	Adults	1 hour
Nightly news	5	Adults/Teenagers	1 hour
Midday news	5	Adults/Teenagers	30 minutes
Super Sleuth Sam	3	Children/Teenagers	1 hour
Life in the Wild	2	Family	1 hour
Cartoon Corner	5	Children	1 hour
Weekend sports	1	Family	30 minutes

EXTENSIONS

- Students can read other texts with timetable formats, such as bus timetables, movie program times, train timetables, etc.
- Students can record their own school or home activities on a timetable format.

WHAT'S ON?

Name _____

Read the the following timetable, which shows a section of the television programs scheduled for weekdays, and answer the questions on the following pages.

Time	Monday	Tuesday	Wednesday	Thursday	Friday
12:00	Midday news	Midday news	Midday news	Midday news	Midday news
12:30	Movie: A Present for Lilly	Movie: The Adventures of Thomas Crumb	Movie: Shootout at Pine Creek	Movie: The Final Flight of Shuttle 9	Movie: Piano Piece for Penny
2:30	Cooking with John	Gardening with Gusto	You Can Make It!	The Reading Club	Renovations Room by Room
3:00	Cartoon Corner	Cartoon Corner	Cartoon Corner	Cartoon Corner	Cartoon Corner
4:00	Life in the Wild	Sporting Heroes	History in the Making	Great Inventions That Changed the World	Life in the Wild
5:00	Super Sleuth Sam	Cops on the Beat	Super Sleuth Sam	Cops on the Beat	Super Sleuth Sam
6:00	Nightly news	Nightly news	Nightly news	Nightly news	Nightly news
7:00	Blue Cove	Blue Cove	Blue Cove	Blue Cove	Blue Cove
7:30	Crazy Squares	Crazy Squares	Crazy Squares	Sport Roundup	Weekend sports
8:00	Inspector Ian	World sports update	Marshall High School	Today's Top Model	Singing Sensations
9:00	Movie: Guys and Dolls	Interview with Don Jones	Movie: Seadogs	Movie: Terry and Clive	Late night football

WHAT'S ON?

Literal   Find the answers directly in the text.

1. Read each sentence. Choose **Yes** or **No**.

   a. The nightly news is on every day. ☐ Yes ☐ No

   b. *Crazy Squares* is on twice. ☐ Yes ☐ No

   c. Shows that tell you how to do things are on at 3:00. ☐ Yes ☐ No

   d. Children can watch cartoons when they get home from school. ☐ Yes ☐ No

   e. Adults can watch a movie while they eat lunch. ☐ Yes ☐ No

   f. Viewers who like sports can watch a show about sports every day. ☐ Yes ☐ No

2. What two times of the day can a person catch up on the latest news?

   _____ and _____

Inferential   Think about what the text says.

1. Write the names of three shows that are on at night specifically for adults to watch.

   • _____

   • _____

   • _____

2. Write the names of two shows that would be very popular with children.

   • _____

   • _____

3. Why are programs that show how to do things usually on at 2:30?

   _____

   _____

WHAT'S ON?

Use what you know about the text and your own experience.

1. Write the name of five shows you watch at home. Next to each name write down what category you think the show belongs to.

	Show	Category
•	_____	_____
•	_____	_____
•	_____	_____
•	_____	_____
•	_____	_____

2. Using the list above, write down the day(s) and time(s) your shows are on.

	Show	Day(s)	Time(s)
•	_____	_____	_____
•	_____	_____	_____
•	_____	_____	_____
•	_____	_____	_____
•	_____	_____	_____

3. Looking at the timetable on page 15, list the shows that you may be interested in viewing.

_____

_____

_____

_____

_____

_____

WHAT'S ON?

Predicting

Use the television program timetable on page 15 to make predictions about some shows.

1. Use your background knowledge about shows you may have seen on television or books you have read to predict what the following shows may be about:

Blue Cove	*Super Sleuth Sam*
Crazy Squares	*The Reading Club*

2. Complete the table to summarize some information from the television program timetable.

Summarizing

Name/type	Number of times aired on weekdays	Suitable audience	Length of show
Daytime movies			
Cops on the Beat			
Nightly news			
Midday news			
Super Sleuth Sam			
Life in the Wild			
Cartoon Corner			
Weekend sports			

Genre: Fable

READING FOCUS

- Analyzes and extracts information from a fable to answer literal, inferential, and applied questions
- Makes connections between an animal character in a traditional fable and a human character of his/her age to write a new fable
- Uses synthesis to write a new fable with the same moral as a traditional fable

ANSWER KEY

Literal (Page 21)

1. He heard some hunters nearby.   2. deer, hunters, fox, lion, rooster

Inferential (Page 21)

1. Answers should indicate that the lion was eating the animals that went into his den.

2. a. Answers will vary. Possible answer(s): We take for granted what we already have.

   b. Answers will vary. Possible answer(s): Be your own person, and do what's right for you.

   c. Answers will vary. Possible answer(s): What may be valuable to one person can be of no value to another.

3.

	Main Character(s)	Setting	Plot Summary
The Deer's Reflection	deer	woods	Deer was complaining about his legs being too long, but his legs actually helped him to run quickly.
The Fox and the Lion	fox and lion	jungle	A lion lured other animals into his cave so that he could eat them. The fox did not fall for his trick and chose to not pay him a visit.
The Rooster and the Jewel	rooster	chicken coop	A rooster searching for food flicked away a beautiful jewel because he valued food more than jewels.

Applied (Page 22)

1–2. Answers will vary.

Applying Strategies (Page 23)

1. a–d. Answers will vary.

2–3. Answers will vary.

EXTENSIONS

- Find fables on the Internet by typing "Aesop's fables" into a search engine. Other well-known authors of fables include Phaedrus, Babrius, Bidpai, and de France.
- After reading various fables, the class can discuss the morals each fable presented.

Name _____

Read the fables and answer the questions on the following pages.

The Deer's Reflection

Once there was a deer who went to drink at a lake. He saw his reflection and thought, "I have beautiful antlers. But my legs are too long."

Just then, the deer heard some hunters nearby. The deer immediately ran into the woods. His long legs helped him to run quickly, but his antlers became caught in the trees.

Moral: Often, we do not realize our own strengths.

The Fox and the Lion

A lion sent a message into the jungle for all the animals to hear. He was sick and would like some visitors in his den. Many animals went, but the fox did not. The next time the fox passed by, the lion called out to him, "Why did you not come to visit me?"

"I decided not to," said the fox. "I noticed that there were many tracks going into your den, but none coming out."

Moral: Don't follow the crowd blindly.

The Rooster and the Jewel

Once there was a rooster who lived in a chicken coop. He used his feet to search for tasty things to eat. One day, he found a beautiful jewel. But he flicked it away and kept hunting for food, thinking, "What bad luck! If only that jewel was a piece of corn instead."

Moral: Beauty is in the eye of the beholder.

THREE FABLES

| **Literal** | Find the answers directly in the text. |

1. Why did the deer run into the woods?

_____

2. List all the characters in the fables.

- _____
- _____
- _____
- _____
- _____

| **Inferential** | Think about what the text says. |

1. Why do you think there were tracks going into the lion's den but no tracks leading out?

_____

_____

2. Explain the moral of each fable in your own words.

   a. Often, we do not realize our own strengths.

   _____

   b. Don't follow the crowd blindly.

   _____

   c. Beauty is in the eye of the beholder.

   _____

3. Complete the table for each of the fables.

	Main Character(s)	Setting	Plot Summary
The Deer's Reflection			
The Fox and the Lion			
The Rooster and the Jewel			

THREE FABLES

1. Which of the animals in the fables do you think was the least clever? Explain why.

_____

_____

_____

_____

_____

_____

_____

2. Which of the three morals on page 20 can you relate to the most? Write about an experience you have had that relates to that particular moral.

_____

_____

_____

_____

_____

_____

_____

_____

_____

Name _____

THREE FABLES

Making Connections

Fables often use animal characters to teach us a lesson or a moral. After reading the fables on page 20, make a connection between a human character and the animal characters.

1. Try changing each main character of two of the fables on page 20 to a human character of your age. The character can be like you or someone you know.

The Deer's Reflection

   a. List three features your character might complain about himself/herself (e.g., too tall, too short).

   _____ _____ _____

   b. Choose one of the features you listed. How could this feature help your character to escape from danger (e.g., being short could help her hide behind a bush)?

   _____

The Fox and the Lion

   c. What could your character's friends choose to do that he/she chooses not to do (e.g., teasing other kids)?

   _____

   d. How could this choice work out well for your character?

   _____

2. Choose one of these fables to rewrite using your human character as the main character. You can change the setting if you wish, but the moral must stay the same.

Synthesizing

I am rewriting the fable: _____

The main character's name is: _____

The new title is: _____

The fable's setting is: _____

3. Use your ideas from Questions 1 and 2 to write your new "human" fable on a separate sheet of paper.

Genre: Recipe

READING FOCUS

- Analyzes and extracts information from a procedure to answer literal, inferential, and applied questions
- Uses sensory imaging to describe what he/she would hear, touch, smell, and taste while making a recipe

ANSWER KEY

Literal (Page 26)

1. You need to beat the egg and chop the butter.

2. eight

3. a. 1 inch   b. 2 handfuls   c. 15 minutes   d. 410°F   e. 12 scones

Inferential (Page 26)

1. Answers should indicate that it means using a spoon to hollow out a hole in the center of the mixture for the milk to be poured into.

2. 2, 4, 1, 3

3. The recipe doesn't call for a leavening agent, so self-rising flour is needed for the dough to rise.

Applied (Page 27)

Answers will vary.

Applying Strategies (Page 28)

1–2. Answers will vary.

EXTENSIONS

- Many books contain collections of recipes suitable for children. Recipes can also be found on the Internet by typing in keywords, such as "recipes for children" or the name of a recipe into a search engine.

- Some simple recipes for children may be found in:
  - *Cool Kids Cook* by Donna Hay
  - *How to Teach Kids to Cook* by Gabriel Gate
  - *Donna Hay Magazine* — Kids issue
  - *There's a Chef in My Soup!* by Emeril Lagasse
  - *Hocus-Pocus Magical Cookbook* by Donna Boundy

Name _____

Read the recipe and answer the questions on the following pages.

Scones

Ingredients

- 3 cups of self-rising flour
- 2 tablespoons of sugar
- 4 tablespoons of butter, chopped
- 1 cup of milk
- 1 egg, beaten
- 2 handfuls of raisins
- butter
- jam

Equipment

- mixing bowl
- wooden spoon
- round cookie cutter
- pastry brush
- sifter
- parchment paper
- baking tray

Method:

1. Sift the flour into a mixing bowl. Mix in the sugar and raisins.

2. Mix the butter into the flour mixture until it looks like breadcrumbs.

3. Use the spoon to make a well in the center of the mixture. Pour in the milk and mix until a sticky dough forms.

4. Put the dough onto a surface sprinkled with flour. Knead the dough until it is smooth.

5. Press and flatten the dough into a shape about an inch thick.

6. Use the cookie cutter to cut the dough into about 12 scones.

7. Place the scones onto the baking tray that is covered with parchment paper.

8. Brush the top of each scone with the beaten egg.

9. Cook the scones in a 410°F oven for 15 minutes.

10. Serve the hot scones with butter and jam.

SCONES

Literal   Find the answers directly in the text.

1. What do you need to do to the egg and the butter before you start making the recipe?

_____

2. How many ingredients do you need for this recipe? _____

3. Answer the following questions.

   a. About how many inches thick should you press the dough? _____

   b. How many handfuls of raisins do you need? _____

   c. How many minutes will the scones take to cook? _____

   d. What temperature does the oven need to be? _____

   e. About how many scones will the recipe make? _____

Inferential   Think about what the text says.

1. What do you think "making a well" might mean?

_____

_____

2. Number these pictures in order from 1 to 4.

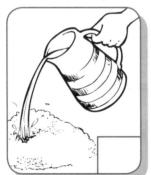   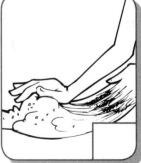

3. Why do you think self-rising flour is used instead of plain flour? _____

_____

SCONES

Write a recipe for making your favorite snack.

Ingredients

- _____
- _____
- _____
- _____
- _____
- _____
- _____

Equipment

- _____
- _____
- _____
- _____
- _____
- _____

Method

_____

_____

_____

_____

_____

_____

_____

_____

_____

_____

_____

SCONES

Sensory Imaging

Sometimes, when we imagine something, we think only about the sense of sight. But what about our other four senses?

1. Imagine you are making the scone recipe from page 25. Choose three of the steps listed under "Method." Write what you might hear, touch, smell, or taste for each one. An example has been done for you.

Step	Description	Senses Described
1	the hard, cold metal of the sifter	touch
	a soft scratching sound while sifting	hearing
	chewing a raisin	taste
	the spoon hitting the bowl while mixing	hearing

2. On a separate sheet of paper, use your descriptions to help you write a poem about making scones.

28

Genre: Science Fiction

READING FOCUS

- Analyzes and extracts information from a science-fiction narrative to answer literal, inferential, and applied questions
- Makes connections between his/her feelings and those of a fictional character
- Predicts the next event to take place in a science-fiction narrative

ANSWER KEY

Literal (Page 31)

1. Answers should include three of the following: He writes in Sivraxian, he has purple hair, he has orange eyes, his family is from the planet Sivrax.

2. a. False   b. False   c. True   d. True

3. His brain was changing and will now only let him write in Sivraxian.

Inferential (Page 31)

1. a. Answers will vary. Possible answer(s): Gavren's mom was wringing her hands because she was nervous about telling Gavren and worried about how he would react.

   b. Answers will vary. Possible answer(s): Miss Whittaker was frowning because she couldn't understand why Gavren was unable to write in English anymore.

   c. Answers will vary. Possible answer(s): Gavren's mouth went dry because he was shocked by what his parents just told him, and his jaw dropped from disbelief.

Applied (Page 32)

Answers will vary.

Applying Strategies (Page 33)

1–3. Answers will vary.

EXTENSIONS

- Some science-fiction novels for children include the following:
  - *The Computer Nut* by Betsy Byars
  - *Animorphs* series by K.A. Applegate
  - *My Teacher Is an Alien* by Bruce Coville

Name _____

Read the science-fiction story and answer the questions on the following pages.

Gavren bit his lip and stared at the wall. His mother and Miss Whittaker were frowning at his latest piece of writing.

Miss Whittaker turned to him. "Gavren, I don't understand."

"I can't seem to help it, Miss Whittaker. It just happens." Gavren looked at the strange symbols he had written. They looked like hieroglyphics. He sighed. He couldn't write in English anymore. Whenever he tried, symbols came out instead.

"Thanks for calling this to my attention, Miss Whittaker," said his mother. She tucked a strand of wiry purple hair back under her beret. "Gavren and I will have a talk at home, and I'll get back to you."

Before Miss Whittaker could reply, his mother had whisked him out the door and headed for the car. She was silent on the drive home. When they arrived, she ushered Gavren into the living room.

"Sit down, Gavren. I'll get your father."

Gavren swallowed. He was in more trouble than he had thought. But when his mother and father walked in, their orange eyes looked sad, not angry.

His father sat next to him. "Gavren, your mother told me about your writing. We didn't think it would happen to you for a few more years yet."

Gavren wrinkled his brow. "What . . . ?"

His mother was wringing her hands. "We should have told you sooner. But it was so hard." She glanced at his father. "Gavren, we're not Earthlings. We're from the planet Sivrax. We came here before you were born, when Sivrax was at war with Goblia. We have brought you up as an Earth boy, but now that you're growing up, it will become harder for you to fit in. You're not going to be able to write in English anymore. Your brain will now only let you write in Sivraxian. And there'll be many other things you'll have to hide . . ."

"Hang on," said Gavren. His mouth was dry. "You're telling me I'm an alien?"

"Yes," said his father. "Haven't you ever wondered why we all have purple hair and orange eyes?"

Gavren touched his wiry hair and thought for a moment. He had always been teased about his looks. Everyone thought he and his parents dyed their hair and wore colored contact lenses.

"So, what happens now?" Gavren asked, his mind whirling.

His father smiled sadly. "Your mother and I think we should move back to Sivrax," he said. "But we won't go unless you want to. What do you think?"

BACK TO SIVRAX?

Literal   Find the answers directly in the text.

1. List three things that make Gavren different from Earth children.

- _____

- _____

- _____

2. Read each sentence. Decide if each statement is **True** or **False**.

    a. Gavren was born on Sivrax.   ☐ True   ☐ False

    b. Miss Whittaker is Gavren's sister.   ☐ True   ☐ False

    c. Sivrax was once at war with Goblia.   ☐ True   ☐ False

    d. Gavren sometimes got teased about his looks.   ☐ True   ☐ False

3. Why couldn't Gavren write in English anymore?

_____

_____

Inferential   Think about what the text says.

1. Why do you think:

    a. Gavren's mom was wringing her hands?

_____

    b. Miss Whittaker was frowning?

_____

    c. Gavren's mouth went dry?

_____

BACK TO SIVRAX?

Applied   Use what you know about the text and your own experience.

What would you say and do if you found out you were an alien? Would you tell anyone?
How would you tell them?

_____

_____

_____

_____

_____

_____

_____

_____

_____

_____

_____

_____

_____

BACK TO SIVRAX?

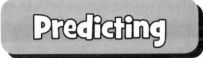

Use the text on page 30 to help you complete this activity.
Gavren's parents give him a week to think about whether
or not he wants to move to Sivrax.

1. Write three important questions you think Gavren should ask his parents about life on Sivrax.
   Write how you think they might reply.

   Question 1: _____

   Reply: _____

   _____

   Question 2: _____

   Reply: _____

   _____

   Question 3: _____

   Reply: _____

   _____

2. Write a list of reasons for and against Gavren leaving Earth.

For Leaving	Against Leaving

3. One week later, Gavren goes to his parents and tells them he has made up his mind. Write
   what he might say to them.

   _____

   _____

   _____

   _____

Genre: Biography

READING FOCUS

- Analyzes and extracts information from a biography to answer literal, inferential, and applied questions
- Makes connections with the characters in a series of books
- Uses synthesis to build up knowledge of particular characters in a series of books

ANSWER KEY

Literal (Page 36)

1. 1897—Enid Blyton was born.

   1922—Her first book was published.

   1938—Her first full-length adventure story, *The Secret Island*, was published.

   1968—Enid Blyton died.

   1995—*Famous Five* series was produced for television.

2. Young Readers—three of the following: *The Faraway Tree, The Wishing Chair, Amelia Jane, Noddy*

   Older Readers—three of the following: *The Famous Five, The Secret Seven, The Five Find-Outers, Barney, Malory Towers, St. Clare's*

Inferential (Page 36)

1. She was trained as a kindergarten teacher and also ran her own elementary school.

2. Answers will vary.

Applied (Page 37)

1–2. Answers will vary.

Applying Strategies (Page 38)

Answers will vary.

EXTENSIONS

- Students can complete a family tree for a chosen series of Enid Blyton books.
- Students can choose a character from a series and write a detailed description.
- Students can make a class list of all the books in each series, and as students complete each one, they record their opinions on a simply-designed book review sheet.

Name _____

Read the biography and answer the questions on the following pages.

Enid Blyton was born in London, England, in 1897. By the time she died, she had written over 600 books and had them translated into almost 70 languages. Since her first book, *Child Whispers*, appeared in 1922, generations of children all over the world have enjoyed her stories.

Enid Blyton trained as a kindergarten teacher and soon opened her own elementary school. She eventually gave up teaching to devote more time to writing children's literature. Her many stories, plays, and songs appeared in *Teachers' World* magazine. They became so popular that teachers used them in their lessons.

In 1938, *The Secret Island* was published. It was the first of many full-length adventure stories. The most popular of these series have been *The Famous Five, The Secret Seven, The Five Find-Outers*, and *Barney* mystery books. The school series, *Malory Towers* and *St. Clare's*, have also been extremely popular.

In 1995, *The Famous Five* series of books was produced for television. This encouraged even more children to pick up her books and start reading.

As well as books for older readers, Enid Blyton wrote many delightful stories for younger children. These include *The Faraway Tree, The Wishing Chair, Amelia Jane*, and *Noddy*.

Enid Blyton died in 1968. She had dedicated her working life to writing books that children would enjoy reading.

For over 90 years, the stories written by Enid Blyton have encouraged children to become enthusiastic readers. They become familiar with the characters in a series and are keen to follow them in the next book. Where will their next adventure take them? How will they solve the latest mystery? What mischief will they get into during the next school year?

To find out, pick up an Enid Blyton book!

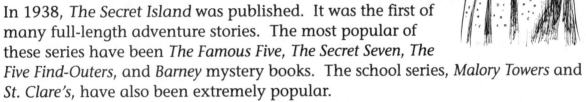

ENID BLYTON

Literal	Find the answers directly in the text.

1. Write the events that occurred in these years:

1897 _____

1922 _____

1938 _____

1968 _____

1995 _____

2. In the boxes below, name three series of books which may be enjoyed by each age group.

Young Readers
- _____
- _____
- _____

Older Readers
- _____
- _____
- _____

Inferential	Think about what the text says.

1. How did Enid Blyton know what sort of work would be useful for teachers when she wrote for *Teachers' World* magazine?

_____

_____

_____

2. Why do you think Enid Blyton chose to write books for children?

_____

_____

_____

ENID BLYTON

Applied   Use what you know about the text and your own experience.

1. Place an **X** in the box next to the opinion(s)/statement(s) with which you agree with regarding a book series.

   ❑ boring—They always have the same characters.

   ❑ great—You really get to know the characters.

   ❑ dull—The same things happen, and you know how each will end.

   ❑ exciting—You wonder how each character will react to different situations.

   ❑ interesting—You have your favorites and can identify with them.

2. *The Famous Five* series was made into a television series. Name a book that you are familiar with that has been made into a movie or television show.

   Title: _____

   a. Which did you like better, the book or the show? Why?

   _____

   _____

   _____

   _____

   b. What are the similarities and the differences between the two?

   _____

   _____

   _____

   _____

   _____

   _____

ENID BLYTON

Most of Enid Blyton's books belong to a series (e.g., *The Famous Five*). Choose a series of books that you are familiar with, and describe two of the main characters.

Series title: _____

Draw a picture of how you imagine each character looks.

Name: _____	Name: _____

For each character, write words and phrases to describe your opinion of his/her personality.

_____

_____

_____

What do you like or dislike most about each character?

_____

_____

_____

Genre: Report

READING FOCUS

- Analyzes and extracts information from a report to answer literal, inferential, and applied questions
- Makes connections between human-caused changes to the environment and the natural world
- Uses synthesis to understand and learn more about the effects of environmental change on a chosen animal

---

ANSWER KEY

Literal (Page 41)

1. global warming

2. a. False   b. True   c. False   d. True   e. True

Inferential (Page 41)

1. a. global warming   drop in polar bear population

    b. longer summers   difficult for polar bears to find food

    c. less sea ice   increased temperatures

    d. less food   sea ice melts sooner and forms later

    e. underweight bears   underweight polar bears

2. The author thinks the population of polar bears will drastically be reduced; extinction is a real possibility.

Applied (Page 42)

1–2. Answers will vary.

Applying Strategies (Page 43)

1. global warming → increased temperatures in Arctic → shorter winters → less sea ice from which to hunt → less food → underweight polar bears → fewer females able to have cubs → drop in polar bear population

2. a–b. Answers will vary.

EXTENSIONS

- Students can write an essay entitled "A Year in the Life of a Polar Bear."
- On a map of the world, students can highlight major areas where environmental change has had a detrimental effect on fauna and flora.
- The class can brainstorm ways they can help to change the tide of environmental damage in their area.

A THREAT TO POLAR BEARS

Name _____

Read the report and answer the questions on the following pages.

Scientists fear that polar bears will be extinct by the end of the 21st century if global warming continues at its present rate. Temperatures are rising more quickly in the Arctic than anywhere else in the world. The Arctic is the only place where polar bears are found. This change to the delicate balance of nature is already having a devastating effect on the health and numbers of the world's population of polar bears.

During the winter, polar bears live and hunt on the sea ice. They roam for many miles in search of their main source of food, the ringed seal. Through the ice, they can sense the movement of a seal below. They lie in wait, close to a hole in the ice, ready to pounce when the seal comes up for air.

In summer, as the ice melts, some bears return to the shore, fasting until the colder weather and sea ice return. Others continue to hunt. They swim in the icy Arctic waters until they reach floating sea ice, from which they can wait for seals to pop to the surface.

Global warming has increased the temperature in the Arctic so much that the warmer weather comes sooner each year and it lasts longer. This means that the sea ice begins melting sooner and takes longer to return. The bears that are fasting have longer to wait before they can begin hunting again. Those that are still hunting on the floating ice have farther to swim between each ice platform.

Polar bears that have been fasting all summer now weigh less and are much weaker. They have lost too much of their fat reserve, which is needed as protection from the cold and is used as a source of energy. Mothers with cubs are unable to produce enough milk, and more cubs are dying. Females who don't weigh enough are unable to have cubs at all.

Predictions are that, by the end of this century, there will be no sea ice left during the longer summertime. As the temperature continues to rise, the cold winter period with abundant sea ice will be much shorter.

All polar bears will be forced to spend the summer months fasting. They will become even weaker and less able to produce and support their young. The population of polar bears will be drastically reduced, making extinction a very real possibility.

A THREAT TO POLAR BEARS

Literal   Find the answers directly in the text.

1. What is believed to be causing temperatures to rise in the Arctic?

_____

_____

2. Read each sentence. Decide if each statement is **True** or **False**.

    a. Polar bears live in the Antarctic.   ☐ True ☐ False

    b. Ringed seal is the polar bear's main source of food.   ☐ True ☐ False

    c. Warmer weather is coming later to the Arctic.   ☐ True ☐ False

    d. Underweight females are unable to have cubs.   ☐ True ☐ False

    e. Bears that fast all summer weigh less and are much weaker.   ☐ True ☐ False

Inferential   Think about what the text says.

1. Match each cause with its effect.

    a. global warming   • drop in polar bear population

    b. longer summers   • difficult for polar bears to find food

    c. less sea ice   • increased temperatures

    d. less food   • sea ice melts sooner and forms later

    e. underweight bears   • underweight polar bears

2. What does the author think about the polar bears' future?

_____

_____

A THREAT TO POLAR BEARS

Applied   Use what you know about the text and your own experience.

1. There are many reasons why global warming is occurring on our planet; some of them are produced or caused by human activities. Complete the table about an animal you know that is endangered due to human actions.

Animal	Humans' Damage	Effect on Animal

2. With a partner, brainstorm some ideas about what actions people can take that would help lessen the impact on animals and their environment.

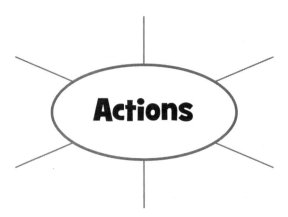

A THREAT TO POLAR BEARS

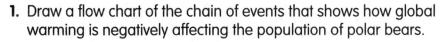

Synthesizing

1. Draw a flow chart of the chain of events that shows how global warming is negatively affecting the population of polar bears.

   Choose one statement for each box.

   - fewer females able to have cubs
   - increased temperatures in Arctic
   - underweight polar bears
   - less food
   - less sea ice from which to hunt
   - shorter winters

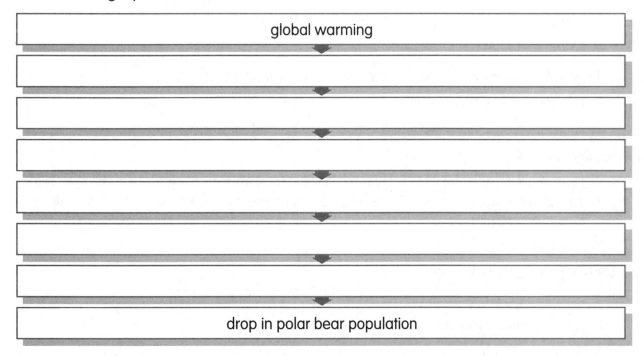

global warming
drop in polar bear population

2. **a.** Draw a flow chart to show how another animal is affected by human-caused environmental damage.

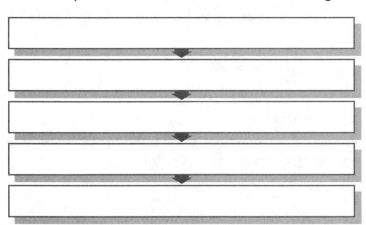

   b. Draw a picture of the animal.

Genre: Play

READING FOCUS

- Analyzes and extracts information from a play to answer literal, inferential, and applied questions
- Compares and makes connections between the moods of characters in a play and how they respond to different stimuli
- Uses synthesis to plan and write a short play, including background and directions, following the format of the text

ANSWER KEY

Literal (Page 46)

1. longbow   2. a fallen branch   3. Merry Men

Inferential (Page 46)

1. Answers will vary. Possible answer(s): He was being sarcastic.

2. a. scoundrel   b. dispute

3. Answers will vary. Possible answer(s): They gained each other's respect.

Applied (Page 47)

1. Answers will vary. Possible answer(s): Robin Hood was grumpy because he was not enjoying the peace; he was bored; he just didn't like people he didn't know; the stranger was mocking him.

2–3. Answers will vary.

Applying Strategies (Page 48)

1. Answers will vary.

2. a–b. Answers will vary.

3. Answers will vary.

EXTENSIONS

- Students can read, review, and act out short plays.
- Students can research the legend of Robin Hood.
- The class can compile a "family tree" of the members of the band of Merry Men, indicating where they came from and under what circumstances they joined.

Name _____

Read the play and answer the questions on the following pages.

Storyteller: Life in Sherwood Forest was too quiet for Robin Hood. For some time, there had been no wealthy strangers passing through for him and the Merry Men to taunt and rob. The men enjoyed this sport of robbing the wealthy and giving to the poor. They especially took pleasure in sending the victim on his way into Nottingham, dressed only in his undergarments. Robin was not enjoying the peace. He was bored.

(Robin steps onto a narrow bridge over a river. As he looks up, he sees a stranger, a giant of a man, about to step onto the bridge at the other end.)

Robin: *(crossly)* Out of the way, you oafish brute! Wait 'til I cross before you step onto the bridge. Can you not see there is room enough for only one person at a time?

Stranger: *(with mock politeness)* Charmed to meet you, oh gracious one. Pray, where did you learn such delightful manners? *(crossly)* I shall not step aside for a fool such as you!

Robin: *(raising his bow)* I'll show you how we solve such disputes here in my country!

Stranger: *(laughing)* What cowardice! You with your longbow while I have nothing but a staff. Hardly a fair fight, oh gracious one!

(Robin lowers his bow and carves himself a staff from a fallen branch.)

Robin: Meet me in the center, and I'll show you a fair fight, you buffoon!

Stranger: "Fair," you say? Let's hope you and I have the same understanding of the word!

(Robin and the stranger fight long and hard, using their weapons to give and receive powerful blows until . . .)

Stranger: Over you go, oh gracious one. Now I shall cross the river in peace.

(Robin is thrown from the bridge into the river below, where he floats away with the current. He swims ashore and blows on his horn. The Merry Men appear, led by Will Stutely.)

Will: What scoundrel has done this to you, sir? Tell us, and we'll fight him.

Robin: No, Will. Save your strength. He is a powerful man.

Stranger: *(laughing)* So glad to hear you say so, oh gracious one!

Robin: *(laughing)* Won't you join us? I am Robin Hood, and these are my Merry Men.

Stranger: I'd be delighted. I'm John, John Little.

Robin: *(laughing)* Welcome to our band, Little John!

LITTLE JOHN

| **Literal** | Find the answers directly in the text. |

1. What weapon was Robin going to use first to settle the dispute?

_____

2. What did Robin use to make his staff? _____

3. What is the name of Robin Hood's band of followers?

_____

| **Inferential** | Think about what the text says. |

1. Why did the stranger call Robin "gracious one"? _____

_____

2. Place an **X** in the box next to the word(s) that has the same meaning as the first.

    a. rogue ☐ oafish brute ☐ buffoon ☐ scoundrel ☐ powerful man

    b. argument ☐ delighted ☐ mock ☐ charmed ☐ dispute

3. Why do you think Robin and the stranger changed their tune?

_____

_____

_____

_____

_____

_____

_____

LITTLE JOHN

Applied   Use what you know about the text and your own experience.

1. Robin had never met the stranger before, yet he was very rude to him. Write possible reasons for his rudeness during their meeting.

_____

_____

_____

_____

_____

2. Do you think Robin Hood and his men are right in robbing wealthy strangers? Explain.

_____

_____

_____

_____

_____

3. Write about a time when you or someone you know gave a wrong, or poor, first impression.

_____

_____

_____

_____

_____

_____

_____

_____

LITTLE JOHN

The storyteller or narrator sets the scene of a play by providing a brief background to the story and any other necessary information. The directions, words in parentheses, indicate the mood of a character, how the actor should read the lines, and any actions he/she must take.

1. On a separate sheet of paper, write a short conversation among three people in which one of them gives a piece of news to the other two.

2. In the boxes below, write:

   a. a brief background to the situation—for example, the relationships among the three people.

   b. directions for each character, including how their moods alter during the conversation and any important movements they make.

Background	**Directions: Character One**
	Directions: Character Two
	Directions: Character Three

3. On a separate sheet of paper, write the conversation as a play script, including the background and all directions.

Genre: Suspense

READING FOCUS

- Analyzes and extracts information from a suspense narrative to answer literal, inferential, and applied questions
- Uses sensory imaging to connect with a character in a text
- Predicts the ending of a suspense story

ANSWER KEY

Literal (Page 51)

1. a. 4   b. 2   c. 1   d. 3
2. Chelsea clenches and unclenches her fists when she is nervous, just as her father does.

Inferential (Page 51)

1. Answers will vary. Possible answer(s): they own a recreational vehicle; they enjoy getting together with their families at the RV park; it's a holiday tradition.
2. a. Answers will vary. Possible answer(s): excited, happy, eager.
   b. Answers will vary. Possible answer(s): worried, nervous, scared, confused.
   c. Answers will vary. Possible answer(s): scared, panicked, frantic, anxious.

Applied (Page 52)

Story Genre: Suspense
Title: Lost!
Characters: Chelsea, Chelsea's family, heavy-footed person
Setting: in the forest near an RV park
Events and Actions: The cousins were playing hide-and-seek. Chelsea hid behind a fallen tree. She realized her cousin wasn't looking for her, and she started to get confused as to her surroundings. She heard a branch being broken by a heavy foot, which sent her to run in a panic. Once she stopped to catch her breath, she came to the realization that she was completely lost.

Applying Strategies (Page 53)

1. a. Answers should include some of the following:
      See—darkness, fallen tree trunk, trees, clouds, bushes, rocks
      Hear—sounds of the night, owl hooting, leaves rustling, crack of the branch being broken by a heavy foot
      Feel—the bark of the fallen tree trunk, the ground, rocks, twigs pulling her hair, sharp prickles from the shrubs
   b. Answers will vary. Possible answer(s): Smell—pine trees, fresh air, woodsy smell
      Taste—nothing; dry mouth from being nervous and running
2. Answers will vary.

EXTENSIONS

- Students can compile lists of authors of suspense stories and explore titles such as the *Goosebumps* series by R.L. Stein.
- Students can write a narrative that uses the five senses to describe how a character is feeling or the setting in which he/she is placed in.

Name _____

Read the suspense story and answer the questions on the following pages.

It started out as a simple game of hide-and-seek with her cousins. They had been playing this game in the forest behind the RV park every Easter and Christmas for years.

This night, the adults were all together celebrating Christmas Eve at the "castle" of all RVs, leaving Chelsea and her cousins with the perfect opportunity to play hide-and-seek in the dark.

Chelsea felt as though she had been hiding behind the fallen tree trunk for hours. Sick of waiting to be found, she began to call out.

"I win, Kit!" she announced to her eldest cousin, the seeker in the game. "I'm over here!"

As Chelsea walked from tree to tree, trying to adjust her eyes to the darkness, she realized she was having trouble determining where "here" was. It was a moonless night, and clouds were covering the stars.

"Hello!" she called again. Chelsea began clenching and unclenching her fists. It was a habit she had picked up from her father—a sign that she was nervous. "How long was I looking for that hiding spot?" she asked herself. "Too long!"

Chelsea stood still and tried to listen to the sounds of the night. If she could hear the music from the Christmas party, she could follow it back to the RV park. Chelsea's brow creased as she concentrated on listening. An owl hooted and the leaves rustled, but no music could be heard.

Crack!

She heard that sound clearly. A small branch was being broken by a heavy foot.

"Kit . . . Is that you?" Chelsea called, her voice quivering slightly.

No reply.

Chelsea decided if it wasn't Kit, then she didn't want to meet whoever was walking around in the forest at night on Christmas Eve, so she began to run.

She charged ahead, dodging trees and bushes, and stumbling over large rocks and branches on the ground. Her hair was being pulled by unfriendly twigs, and her bare legs scratched by sharp prickles in the shrubs.

Chelsea looked left and right, making instant decisions about which direction to take. Her heart was beating so rapidly she could feel her pulse pounding in her neck. She gasped and tried to ignore the twisting feeling in her stomach.

Her body finally said "Enough!," so she stopped running and leaned against a tree. When she had caught her breath, Chelsea cautiously lifted her head and scanned her surroundings. The forest was denser than she had ever seen, and it felt colder than before, too. Now she was completely lost . . .

LOST!

> **Literal**   Find the answers directly in the text.

1. Put these events in order from 1 to 4.

    a. _____ Chelsea's legs are scratched, and her hair is pulled.

    b. _____ Chelsea hears an owl hooting.

    c. _____ Chelsea enters the forest to hide.

    d. _____ A branch is broken by a heavy foot.

2. What habit had Chelsea copied from her father?

    _____

    _____

    _____

> **Inferential**   Think about what the text says.

1. Why do you think Chelsea and her family are staying in the RV park? Give reasons for your answer.

    _____

    _____

2. How do you think Chelsea was feeling when:

    a. she was looking for a hiding spot?

    _____

    b. she realized Kit wasn't looking for her anymore?

    _____

    c. she was running through the forest, away from the person who stepped on the branch?

    _____

LOST!

Applied   Use what you know about the text and your own experience.

Complete each of the fields in the table for the story "Lost!"

Story Genre:	Title:
Characters	**Events and Actions**
Setting	

52

Name _____

LOST!

Sensory Imaging

Use the text on page 50 to help you complete this activity. To help readers connect to a character in a story, writers often use the senses to describe what a character is experiencing. Our senses are sight, taste, touch, sound, and smell.

1. **a.** Reread the story. Highlight the sentences or phrases that use the senses to describe what Chelsea is feeling. Record your findings below.

What can she see?	What can she hear?	What can she feel?

b. Use your imagination to answer the next two questions.

What can Chelsea smell? _____

_____

What can Chelsea taste? _____

_____

Predicting

2. Complete the story.

Now Chelsea was completely lost . . . _____

_____

_____

_____

_____

_____

Genre: Mystery

READING FOCUS

- Analyzes and extracts information from a mystery to answer literal, inferential, and applied questions
- Uses sensory imaging to set the scene of a story
- Determines the important features of a description

ANSWER KEY

Literal (Page 56)

1. a. 2   b. 4   c. 3   d. 1
2. Thomas, Joe, Ellie, Jodie

Inferential (Page 56)

1. Answers will vary. Possible answer(s): to enjoy the warmth, a hot meal, and a roaring log fire.
2. a. The friends could not see clearly because the fog was too thick for them to see things in the distance.

   b. A man had caught an injured badger to take back to his cabin so that he could treat the badger's injuries and give it some tender, loving care.

Applied (Page 57)

1. Answers will vary. Possible answer(s): another animal could have attacked the badger; it got caught in a trap; it stepped on something sharp.
2. Answers will vary. Possible answer(s): compassionate, loving, caring, heroic, tender.
3. Answers will vary.

Applying Strategies (Page 58)

1. Time of day: dusk
   Conditions outside: foggy, cold, thick snow on the ground
   How the character(s) are feeling: intrigued, curious, amazed
2. Answers will vary.
3. Answers will vary. Possible answer(s): to give the reader a mental image of what's happening in the story.
4. Answers will vary.

EXTENSIONS

- Students can research other animal species that are threatened by poaching and baiting.
- The class can gather mystery stories from a range of authors.
- Students can read stories involving the relationships between people and animals; for example:
  - *Black Beauty* by Anna Sewell
  - *In Flanders Fields* by Norman Jorgensen
  - *One Unhappy Horse* by C.S. Adler
  - *Saving Lilly* by Peg Kehret
  - *Star in the Storm* by Joan Hiatt Harlow

MYSTERY IN THE NIGHT

Name _____

Read the mystery story and answer the questions on the following pages.

The fog was beginning to come down as the four friends trudged home through the snow. As they spoke, their warm breath mixed with the cold, crisp air, sending out puffs like smoke signals. They would all be glad to reach the lodge and enjoy the warmth of a hot meal and a roaring log fire. Suddenly, a piercing cry rang out, shattering the peace of the early evening.

"What on Earth was that?" demanded Thomas, as he broke away from the group and headed toward the edge of the woods, where he thought the noise had come from.

"Sounded like a wild animal to me," shuddered Joe. "Let's check it out."

"Wait!" cried Ellie. "Over there! Look!"

Four pairs of eyes strained to make out the outline of a shadowy figure in the distance. They all kept very still, watching as the figure came toward them. It stopped a short distance away. They saw it bend down. It looked as though it was fighting with itself. The cry came again. The sound of terror sent a chill down their spines. The figure rose slowly, this time with what looked like a large, struggling sack across its back. It began to make its way back through the woods.

"We must follow it. I need to know what it's doing," insisted Jodie.

The others were not keen to postpone a hot meal, but they couldn't leave their friend to play detective on her own. They plodded silently through the snow, keeping a safe distance behind their target. The figure led them to a log cabin in a clearing. They watched as it opened the door and took the sack inside.

As the lights went on, they could clearly see what was happening. With their noses pressed against a window, they watched a young man gently coax a terrified animal out of the sack. As he tenderly muttered words of encouragement, a black-and-white-striped snout began to appear. One of its front paws was badly cut. The badger must have been in terrible pain, yet it allowed the man to bathe and bandage it.

"Wow!" echoed the friends, one after the other.

"He must be a wizard." whispered Joe in admiration. "You'd think the badger would have attacked him, but it's as gentle as a lamb."

MYSTERY IN THE NIGHT

Literal   Find the answers directly in the text.

1. Put these events in order from 1 to 4.

    a. _____ Thomas headed toward the edge of the woods.

    b. _____ The man coaxed the badger out of the sack.

    c. _____ Jodie wanted to follow the figure.

    d. _____ A piercing cry rang out.

2. Write the names of the four friends.

    • _____   • _____

    • _____   • _____

Inferential   Think about what the text says.

1. Why were the friends keen to get home?

    _____

    _____

    _____

2. **It looked as though it was fighting with itself.**

    a. From the excerpt above, explain why the friends could not see clearly.

    _____

    _____

    b. Explain what was actually happening.

    _____

    _____

MYSTERY IN THE NIGHT

Applied   Use what you know about the text and your own experience.

1. How do you think the badger might have received its injury?

_____

_____

_____

_____

_____

2. Write several words to describe the man's actions.

_____   _____

_____   _____

_____   _____

_____   _____

3. The group of friends decided to investigate the situation. What would you have done, and would you have handled it differently if you were by yourself?

_____

_____

_____

_____

_____

_____

_____

_____

_____

_____

MYSTERY IN THE NIGHT

Determining Importance

A good writer always sets the scene of a story. Use the text on page 55 to help you complete the following activity.

1. Find words or phrases from the text that set the scene of the story.

Time of day:	Conditions outside:
How the character(s) are feeling:	

2. In a similar way, set the scene for a story of your own.

Time of day:	Conditions outside:
How the character(s) are feeling:	

3. Why do you think setting the scene is important?

_____

_____

4. Choose a story you have read, and write a description of a scene from the story.

Author: _____

Scene: _____

_____

_____

_____

Genre: Humor

READING FOCUS

- Analyzes and extracts information from a humorous narrative to answer literal, inferential, and applied questions

- Uses sensory imaging to describe how he/she might feel about and react to situations experienced by a fictional character

- Makes connections between the feelings and reactions of a fictional character and his/her own feelings and reactions

ANSWER KEY

Literal (Page 61)

1. She thought he was telling Mrs. Tan about her allergies.

2. a. False   b. False   c. True   d. True

Inferential (Page 61)

1. Emma had overheard Tilda's father saying that the dog was "our Princess," but because of his accent, she thought he was saying that Tilda was a princess. The rumor spread around the class.

2. She realized that all the students thought she was a princess, and she decided to enjoy the attention while it lasted.

Applied (Page 62)

1–2. Answers will vary.

Applying Strategies (Page 63)

Answers will vary.

EXTENSIONS

- Students may also enjoy reading the following humorous books.
  - *Paul Jennings' Funniest Stories* by Paul Jennings
  - *The Twist* by Roald Dahl
  - *The 26-Story Treehouse* by Andy Griffiths

THE NEW GIRL

Name _____

Read the humorous story and answer the questions on the following pages.

"Class, this is our new friend, Tilda. She comes all the way from Sweden. Tilda's dad wants to have a quick chat with me outside, so keep working quietly."

Tilda sat down and picked her nails. She hated starting at a new school. Before long, she would be teased about her name and her accent.

A scuffling noise made her look up. A girl had moved to the window and had pressed her ear up against the screen. She grinned. "Let's find out what's so private about the new girl." She poked out her tongue at Tilda, making some of the class laugh.

Tilda bit her lip and frowned. Her father was probably in the middle of telling her new teacher about her allergies. It was embarrassing. Sometimes, he treated her like a baby. To make matters worse, he had brought their dog with him on the walk to the school. Most kids laughed when they saw her. She looked just like a fluffy cotton ball with legs.

Tilda glanced at the girl, waiting for the teasing to start. But she was startled by what she saw. The girl's mouth was open, and she was staring at Tilda.

"Is—is that true?" the girl stammered. "Are you really a—?"

"Emma! Back to your desk, please!" Mrs. Tan appeared in the doorway. With wide eyes, the girl slunk to her chair, still gawking at Tilda.

Puzzled, Tilda tried to concentrate on the lesson. What on Earth had her father said to Mrs. Tan?

All morning, the class was alive with whispers. Whenever Tilda looked around, someone would be gazing at her as if she was famous. At recess, she was even more confused when she was surrounded by the class. Everyone was chattering excitedly.

One girl tugged at her shirt. "Where's your crown?"

Tilda wrinkled her brow. "What? My crown? What are you talking about?"

"I thought every princess owned a crown." The girl sounded disappointed.

Princess? Then, in a flash, everything suddenly made sense. Of course. Her father wouldn't have just talked about her allergies that morning. He was so proud of the dog that he always told everyone her name.

"She is our Princess," he would say. But with a Swedish accent, Tilda realized, that sentence might just sound like "She is a princess."

Tilda suppressed a grin and put her nose in the air. "I had to leave my crown behind in Sweden. But I'm sure it will be sent on. Excuse me, please."

She began to laugh as she stalked regally to the girls' bathroom. She was sure everyone would find out the truth eventually. But until then, she was going to have some fun as Her Royal Highness, Princess Tilda of Sweden.

THE NEW GIRL

Literal Find the answers directly in the text.

1. What did Tilda first think her father was saying to Mrs. Tan?

_____

_____

_____

2. Read each sentence. Decide if each statement is **True** or **False**.

    a. Tilda liked starting at a new school.   ☐ True ☐ False

    b. Tilda's father was the king of Sweden.   ☐ True ☐ False

    c. Tilda's dog made most children laugh.   ☐ True ☐ False

    d. Emma listened to the conversation between Mrs. Tan and Tilda's father.   ☐ True ☐ False

Inferential Think about what the text says.

1. Explain why the class thought Tilda was a princess.

_____

_____

_____

2. Why do you think Tilda was laughing at the end of the story?

_____

_____

_____

_____

THE NEW GIRL

Applied   Use what you know about the text and your own experience.

1. Imagine you were new to the school, and everyone believed that you were a prince or princess. Would you let them know the truth or enjoy living as royalty for a while? What would you say to the students?

_____

_____

_____

_____

_____

_____

_____

_____

_____

_____

2. If you found out that someone at your school was a prince or princess, would you treat them differently? Give reasons for your answer.

_____

_____

_____

_____

_____

_____

_____

THE NEW GIRL

Making Connections

Use the text on page 60 to help you complete this activity. Tilda goes through many emotions in this story. Put yourself in her place. How would you feel about and react to each of the situations she found herself in?

Situation	Feelings	Reactions (e.g., biting nails, shaking, talking loudly)
It is your first day of school in a new country. You have an unusual name and accent. Your teacher is introducing you to the class.		
One of your new classmates starts to listen in on a private conversation about you.		
Your new class begins to stare at you and whisper as if you were famous. You have no idea why.		
You realize that your new classmates think you are a prince or princess.		

Genre: Legend

READING FOCUS

- Analyzes and extracts information from a legend to answer literal, inferential, and applied questions
- Determines importance of events within a story
- Summarizes the key events of a story

ANSWER KEY

Literal (Page 66)

1. grave of Gelert
2. in a hunting lodge in the valleys below the mountains of North Wales

Inferential (Page 66)

1. Gelert was on the scent of a wild animal, so for him to suddenly stop dead in his tracks and race back to the lodge was out of character.
2. He was proud of himself that he saved the baby from harm.
3. He realized he made a terrible mistake when he saw his baby was unharmed and when the servant found the gray wolf.

Applied (Page 67)

1. Answers will vary.
2. a–c. Answers will vary.

Applying Strategies (Page 68)

1. a–f. Answers will vary for each box but should include the following events:
   - Prince Llewelyn, his wife, and Gelert went out to hunt and left the baby with a nursemaid.
   - Gelert rushed back toward the lodge, and Llewelyn and Llewelyn's wife followed Gelert back.
   - They discovered Gelert with red stain and their baby missing from his cradle.
   - Llewelyn reacted and mortally injured Gelert.
   - They realized the baby was unharmed.
   - A servant discovered the body of a large gray wolf.
   - Llewelyn realized the mistake he made.
   - Gelert had a hero's burial.
2. Drawings will vary.

EXTENSIONS

- Students can look for other stories in which they can identify with the actions of the characters and in which an animal proves to be a loyal friend.
- Students can conduct research on the Internet for legends from around the world.
- Students can record references from literature and indicate how places gained their names.

Name _____

Read the Welsh legend and answer the questions on the following pages.

Many, many years ago, the valleys below the mountains of North Wales were inhabited only by wildflowers and animals. The only building for miles around was a hunting lodge in a forest clearing. Prince Llewelyn and his wife, Princess Joan, came to stay at the lodge, as they were both very fond of hunting. One day, leaving their baby son in the care of the nursemaid, Llewelyn and Joan went out to hunt.

Llewelyn's bravest and most faithful dog, Gelert, was first on the scent of a wild animal. Suddenly, he turned and raced back toward the lodge. Llewelyn and Joan wondered why their dog was behaving so strangely. They decided to leave the hunt and follow Gelert.

As they arrived at the lodge, Gelert came running from the house to meet them, his jaws stained with red and his tail wagging. Llewelyn stormed into the house. He fell upon a horrifying sight, when he set his eyes on his son's empty cradle.

In a rage, Llewelyn reacted and mortally injured Gelert. How could such a trusted friend harm his only child?

Suddenly, Llewelyn heard a muffled cry. A blanket on the floor beside him began to move. Using his sword, Llewelyn carefully pulled back the blanket and saw his young son, safe and unharmed. At that moment, a servant gave a loud cry. He had found the body of a large gray wolf. The wolf's injuries revealed that he had been attacked by a dog.

Llewelyn sank to his knees in despair beside his loyal companion. Bitter tears ran down his face as he realized what he had done. He looked at his child, happy now in his mother's arms, but his own heart was heavy with grief.

He gave orders for the brave Gelert to be given a hero's burial and for a large stone to be raised above his grave. On the stone, the story would be inscribed, telling how brave, faithful Gelert saved his master's child from the wolf and of how that master, in haste, mortally wounded his most loyal friend.

Today, in the town of Beddgelert, which in English means "grave of Gelert," you can still see the large stone above the grave that tells the sad story: the story of Gelert.

THE STORY OF GELERT

Literal Find the answers directly in the text.

1. What does the Welsh name "Beddgelert" mean in English?

_____

_____

2. Where were Prince Llewelyn and his family staying?

_____

_____

Inferential Think about what the text says.

1. What was so strange about Gelert's behavior that Prince Llewelyn thought he should follow him?

_____

_____

_____

2. Why do you think Gelert was wagging his tail?

_____

_____

_____

3. When did Prince Llewelyn realize he had made a terrible mistake?

_____

_____

_____

THE STORY OF GELERT

Applied   Use what you know about the text and your own experience.

1. Where do you think the nursemaid might have gone?

_____

_____

_____

2. Have you ever reacted badly to a situation and then realized you were in the wrong?

   a. What was the situation?

   _____

   _____

   _____

   _____

   b. Who else was involved?

   _____

   _____

   c. How did you resolve the situation?

   _____

   _____

   _____

   _____

   _____

Name _____

THE STORY OF GELERT

Use the text on page 65 to help you summarize the story.

1. In a story, key events are the parts that cannot be left out without changing the story. In the boxes, write the key events as they occur in "The Story of Gelert." There are more than six events, but some belong together. You decide which these are.

a.	b.	c.
d.	e.	f.

2. Draw and label a picture to illustrate a part of "The Story of Gelert."

Genre: Journal

READING FOCUS

- Analyzes and extracts information from a journal to answer literal, inferential, and applied questions
- Determines and uses the important information in a journal entry to complete a table

ANSWER KEY

Literal (Page 71)

1. True   2. False   3. False   4. False   5. False   6. True

Inferential (Page 71)

1. Kublai Khan was descended from a family of fierce warriors.
2. Kublai Khan encouraged foreigners to visit.
3. Kublai Khan used men from other countries to help govern China.
4. Kublai Khan extended highways and repaired buildings.
5. Kublai Khan allowed the people to follow their own religions.
6. Kublai Khan wasted a lot of money running his empire.

Applied (Page 72)

1. Answers will vary. Possible answer(s): There was a great distance to travel between the countries, which may have weakened the Mongol army; it would have cost more money for food, equipment, etc.; they may not have had ships to use, etc.

2. Answers will vary.

Applying Strategies (Page 73)

Name: Kublai Khan		
Main Achievements		**Most Memorable Failures**
• Unified Mongolia and China • First foreign ruler of China • Founded the Yuan dynasty • Included Chinese traditions in government • Created a multinational government	• Rebuilt Grand Canal • Extended highways • Encouraged Chinese art and thinking • Established Buddhism as state religion • Encouraged foreign trade and visitors	• Failed to conquer Japan, Myanmar, Vietnam, and Indonesia, and lost a lot of money in the process • New paper currency failed • Spent extravagantly on trying to run the country

EXTENSIONS

- Students can keep a weekly journal of school and home activities.
- Students can read stories such as *The Adventures of Tom Sawyer* and *The Adventures of Huckleberry Finn*, which detail events in the lives of the main characters.
- Students can keep an art journal.

THE JOURNAL OF KUBLAI KHAN

Name _____

Read the extract from the journal of Kublai Khan and answer the questions on the following pages.

Winter 1292

Today as I sit on my throne in Cambaluc—the center of my empire—I find myself contemplating the events that led to my rise as leader of this great Mongol Empire. I wonder if my grandfather, Genghis Khan, would approve of my changes or whether he would think that I had wasted my time, men, and energy for a useless dream.

Life has not always been easy. Every battle takes its toll on a warrior's physical and mental strength, but I have kept my eyes firmly fastened on my goal to unify Mongolia and China. I am the first foreigner to be ruler of China. The Sung Empire has been replaced by my own Yuan dynasty. A new era has begun!

I have had successes and failures along the way. My successes have often come at a cost. I have lost family and friends in fierce battles. My own brother, Mongke, died long ago in battle. It seems like yesterday, even though it was over thirty years ago.

I have tried to use my intellect, as well as my strength, to leave a legacy for future generations. I have attempted to fit Chinese traditions into my government. As the Chinese seem to lack the ability to govern properly, I have also recruited men from different nations to help. I have rebuilt the Grand Canal to help trade, repaired granaries and other public buildings, and extended highways. I have encouraged Chinese art and educators. I have established Buddhism as the state religion and allowed other religions to be practiced. I encouraged foreigners to trade with us. The European Marco Polo, a well-known traveler, became a frequent visitor to our capital city. He even told stories about our way of life to his countrymen.

My failures will always remain a great source of frustration to me. My two attempts to conquer Japan failed, as did wars in Myanmar, Vietnam, and Indonesia. I should never have yielded to pressure from my Mongol advisers. Instead, I should have heeded my own "gut" feelings about these situations. The financial cost of these expeditions was great and caused hardship within the empire. The new paper currency I tried to introduce was also a failure. I fear I have been extravagant at times, spending money on new projects and trying to run the empire. My only excuse is that I know that life can be short, and I hasten to use the time I have left to do everything I want to do!

I wonder if future dynasties will learn from my failures and applaud my successes. Only the passage of time will tell how I will be remembered!

THE JOURNAL OF KUBLAI KHAN

Literal Find the answers directly in the text.

Read each sentence. Decide if each statement is **True** or **False**.

1. Khublai Khan was the grandson of Genghis Khan. ☐ True ☐ False

2. Everything Kublai Khan did was successful. ☐ True ☐ False

3. Kublai Khan cared only about war and fighting. ☐ True ☐ False

4. Kublai Khan's goal was to conquer the whole world. ☐ True ☐ False

5. Kublai Khan wanted to completely change the countries he conquered. ☐ True ☐ False

6. Kublai Khan established a new dynasty. ☐ True ☐ False

Inferential Think about what the text says.

Draw lines to match the beginning of the sentence to its ending.

1. Kublai Khan was descended from a family • running his empire.

2. Kublai Khan encouraged foreigners • to follow their own religions.

3. Kublai Khan used men from other countries • to visit.

4. Kublai Khan extended highways • to help govern China.

5. Kublai Khan allowed the people • and repaired buildings.

6. Kublai Khan wasted a lot of money • of fierce warriors.

THE JOURNAL OF KUBLAI KHAN

Applied   Use what you know about the text and your own experience.

1. With a partner, discuss and write reasons why Kublai Khan's plans to conquer Japan, Myanmar, and Indonesia may have failed. Use an atlas to find some clues.

   _____

   _____

   _____

   _____

   _____

   _____

2. "Kublai Khan was a great leader of the Mongol Empire."

   If you agree with this statement, what attributes did Kublai Khan possess that made him a great leader? If you disagree with this statement, support your opinion with specifics of why he was not a great leader.

   _____

   _____

   _____

   _____

   _____

   _____

   _____

   _____

   _____

THE JOURNAL OF KUBLAI KHAN

Determining Importance

Famous people from history are remembered for their achievements and failures. Complete the first table using the text from page 70. Then, select another well-known person of your own to complete the second table.

Name: Kublai Khan	Name:
Main Achievements	**Main Achievements**
Most Memorable Failures	**Most Memorable Failures**

Genre: Letters

READING FOCUS

- Analyzes and extracts information from three letters to answer literal, inferential, and applied questions
- Scans text to locate specific information
- Synthesizes information from a text to deduce its purpose and style

---

ANSWER KEY

Literal (Page 76)

1. a. birthday   b. work   c. bars   d. machine   e. Abbot   f. principal
2. email address, home address, phone number

Inferential (Page 76)

1. She stated in her letter that the unhealthy food should be removed from its shelves. She also stated that she would be taking the matter to the next parents' meeting.
2. Three of the following:
   - Letter 1 uses the greeting "Hello," and letter 3 uses "Dear."
   - Letter 1 was handwritten, and letter 3 was typed out.
   - Letter 1 closes the letter with "Lots of love," and letter 3 closes with "Yours sincerely,."
   - Letter 1 is informal and personal, and letter 3 is formal and written using a business-letter format.

Applied (Page 77)

1. Answers will vary. Possible answer(s): She lives far away and was unable to attend the party.
2. Answers will vary.

Applying Strategies (Page 78)

1.

	Letter 1	Letter 2	Letter 3
Written by	Nicola	Mrs. T. West (a parent)	Oliver Wood
Written to	Nanna	Mr. Ladel (the principal)	Personnel handling the hire
Greeting (Dear, etc.)	Hello Nanna,	Dear Mr. Ladel,	Dear Sir/Madam,
Closing (From, etc.)	Lots of love,	Regards,	Yours sincerely,
Purpose (Why was it written?)	to tell Nanna about her birthday party and to thank her for the gift	to communicate with the principal her opinion on the food selection and what should be done about it	to express his interest in the job opening

2. Letter 1—Informal; check for accuracy regarding the sentence from the letter
   Letter 2—Formal; check for accuracy regarding the sentence from the letter
   Letter 3—Formal; check for accuracy regarding the sentence from the letter

---

EXTENSIONS

- Discuss with the class the use of emails instead of handwritten letters. Students can create a survey that asks the viewpoint of others, such as teachers, siblings, parents, and grandparents, etc. Students can compile their data and present their findings to another class.

LETTERS FOR A PURPOSE

Name _____

Read the letters and answer the questions on the following pages.

Hello Nanna,

Thank you for the horse book. I love it! It arrived exactly on my birthday, too! The mailman knocked on the door and gave it to me because it wouldn't fit in the mailbox.

My party was a "pink party" with pink balloons, a pink cake, and pink lollipops! We played games and sang, using my new karaoke machine. It was so much fun!

Wish you could have been there.

Lots of love,

Nicola XXXX

1

Attn: Principal Ladel

Tuesday, May 31, 2015

Dear Mr. Ladel,

I was astounded and shocked yesterday after emptying Trent's school bag and finding a soda can, two candy bar wrappers, and the wrapper of an ice-cream bar!

It is time the cafeteria at Thornton Elementary caught up with the rest of the country and removed these unhealthy foods from its shelves!

I will be taking this matter to the next parents' meeting.

Regards,
Mrs. T. West

2

23 Fiddle Drive
Bridgeman, WA 60608
Ph: 988-0111
bwoods@email.com

April 12, 2015

TOYS2TOYS
20 Abbot Road
Balcatta, WA 60521

Dear Sir/Madam,

I would like to express my interest in the position of store manager that was advertised in the *Times* paper on Saturday, April 10. Please send me the information pack and appropriate forms.

Yours sincerely,

Oliver Wood

Mr. Oliver Wood

3

LETTERS FOR A PURPOSE

Store
Manager
Toys2Toys

Literal   Find the answers directly in the text.

1. Complete the sentences using the words in the box.

| work | Abbot | principal | machine | bars | birthday |

   a. Nicola has just celebrated her _____.

   b. Oliver Wood would like to _____ at TOYS2TOYS.

   c. Trent bought an ice-cream bar, candy _____, and soda from the cafeteria.

   d. Nicola received a karaoke _____ for her birthday.

   e. TOYS2TOYS is found at 20 _____ Road in Balcatta.

   f. Mr. Ladel is the _____ at Trent's school.

2. List three pieces of contact information Oliver Wood gave to the TOYS2TOYS company in his letter.

   • _____

   • _____

   • _____

Inferential   Think about what the text says.

1. How do you know Mrs. T. West is unhappy with the food sold at the cafeteria?

   _____

2. Letter 3 to TOYS2TOYS and letter 1 to Nicola's nanna have been written differently. List three differences between the letters.

   • _____

   • _____

   • _____

LETTERS FOR A PURPOSE

Use what you know about the text and your own experience.

1. Why do you think Nicola's nanna sent her birthday present through the mail?

   _____

   _____

   _____

   _____

   _____

   _____

   _____

2. Should unhealthy foods be banned from school cafeterias?   ☐ Yes ☐ No

   Why? _____

   _____

   _____

   _____

   _____

   _____

   _____

   _____

   _____

   _____

   _____

   _____

Name _____

LETTERS FOR A PURPOSE

Use the text on page 75 to help you complete this activity.

1. Complete the table.

	Letter 1	Letter 2	Letter 3
Written By			
Written To			
Greeting (Dear etc.)			
Closing (From etc.)			
Purpose (Why was it written?)			

Formal letters follow a set of rules for structure and often say only what needs to be done. Informal letters are written to someone you know well and use casual, friendly words.

Synthesizing

2. Decide if the letters are formal or informal, and copy a sentence from each one as an example of the language used.

Letter 1	Letter 2	Letter 3
☐ Formal ☐ Informal	☐ Formal ☐ Informal	☐ Formal ☐ Informal
_____	_____	_____
_____	_____	_____
_____	_____	_____
_____	_____	_____
_____	_____	_____

Genre: Review

READING FOCUS

- Analyzes and extracts information from a review to answer literal, inferential, and applied questions
- Scans a text to find information to complete a list of facts
- Determines the importance of information in a text to write from a fictional character's point of view

---

ANSWER KEY

Literal (Page 81)

1. one hour

2. Two of the following: the guitarist couldn't get any sound out of his guitar, the drummer dropped her drumsticks twice, and the lead singer had to leave the stage for 10 minutes.

3. The audience's applause became less enthusiastic, as they were not familiar with the songs.

Inferential (Page 81)

Answers will vary.

Applied (Page 82)

1. Answers will vary. Possible answer(s):

   For—you expect to be entertained especially if you paid for it, it gives the performers feedback

   Against—it's rude, people should still clap politely, shows bad manners, hurts the feelings of the performers

2. Answers will vary. Possible answer(s): good lead singer, talented musicians, good music that people know, good weather, crowd with a positive energy, good sound system, great venue.

Applying Strategies (Page 83)

1. Six of the following: all-around disappointment, plagued with problems, singer's voice was croaky and out of tune, shouldn't have bothered to battle on, songs were awful, the songs were slow and dreary with boring lyrics, audience's applause was less enthusiastic, only positive thing was that the concert was short, audience was angry, referred to the concert as "last night's disaster," find themselves with a hugely reduced fan club.

2. Answers will vary. Possible answer(s): having technical difficulties, it was our first show at the venue, feeling under the weather.

3. Answers will vary.

EXTENSIONS

- Students can read concert, movie, and book reviews that can be found in newspapers and on the Internet.

CONCERT "ALL-ROUND DISAPPOINTMENT"

Name _____

Read the review and answer the questions on the following pages.

Even diehard fans of pop supergroup Tiger Tail would have to agree that last night's concert at the Maynard Theater was an all-round disappointment.

From the moment the band members arrived on stage, they were plagued with problems. During the first song, guitarist Ben Vicary couldn't get any sound out of his guitar, and Sharon Mullane dropped her drumsticks twice. Lead singer Shane Crosby also had to leave the stage for 10 minutes because of what he claimed were "throat problems." His voice was croaky and out of tune for the rest of the night.

Despite the problems, the group battled on but probably shouldn't have bothered. They chose to play many songs from an upcoming album, which the audience was not familiar with. And most of these songs were truly awful. They all seemed to be slow and dreary with boring lyrics. Many of them sounded the same. The audience's applause became less enthusiastic with every passing minute.

The only positive thing that can be said about the concert is that it was short. The band stayed on stage for one hour—the shortest concert I have ever been to. Many in the crowd were not impressed by this. There were angry shouts and boos for several minutes after the band left the stage.

Tiger Tail has two more concerts left to play at the Maynard Theater. Let's hope that the band members improve on last night's disaster, or they may find themselves with a hugely reduced fan club.

—Oscar Crisp

CONCERT "ALL-ROUND DISAPPOINTMENT"

Literal   Find the answers directly in the text.

1. How long did the band stay on stage?

_____

2. Name two things that happened during the first song.

- _____

  _____

- _____

  _____

3. What problem did playing songs from the upcoming album cause?

_____

_____

_____

Inferential   Think about what the text says.

Do you think this is a fair review?   ☐ Yes   ☐ No

Give reasons for your answer.

_____

_____

_____

_____

_____

Name _____ Activities

CONCERT "ALL-ROUND DISAPPOINTMENT"

Applied Use what you know about the text and your own experience.

1. "It is okay for people to boo and shout after a performance they didn't enjoy."

   Write a list of points for and against this statement.

For	Against

2. List six things you think would make for a good concert.

   • _____
   • _____
   • _____
   • _____
   • _____
   • _____

CONCERT "ALL-ROUND DISAPPOINTMENT"

Scanning

Scan the text on page 80 to locate the negative remarks made by the critic.

1. Oscar Crisp, the reviewer, did not seem to enjoy the concert at all. List six negative things he wrote about it.

- _____

  _____

- _____

  _____

- _____

  _____

- _____

  _____

- _____

  _____

- _____

  _____

2. Imagine you are the lead singer of Tiger Tail. Write three excuses for your terrible concert.

Synthesizing

- _____

  _____

- _____

  _____

- _____

  _____

3. Imagine you are the manager of Tiger Tail. You have just read Crisp's review. What advice would you give to the band to help them improve their future performances?

_____

_____

_____

_____

Genre: Fantasy

READING FOCUS

- Analyzes and extracts information from a fantasy text to answer literal, inferential, and applied questions
- Scans text to find specific words and clues to help write definitions

ANSWER KEY

Literal (Page 86)

1. in Alice's garden
2. Three of the following: tiny lanterns strung between flowers and tree stumps; bright lights buzzing around his ankles; winged fairies of different colors dancing around a blazing fire; beautiful white fairy with delicate, gossamer wings and eyes as bright as sapphires; flat pebbles covered with spider-web tablecloths; petal plates filled with grass-seed cookies.

Inferential (Page 86)

1. "His eyes opened wide in amazement;" ". . . gazed in wonder . . ."
2. Answers will vary.

Applied (Page 87)

1–2. Answers will vary.

Applying Strategies (Page 88)

Word	Clues	Definition
exhausted	playing all afternoon	tired
wispy	wispy clouds floating gently	thin, delicate
slithered	crawling through a tunnel	slid
amazement	his eyes opened wide	shock, wonder
gossamer	delicate	sheer, delicate
crouched	crouched down	bent down
gazed	gazed in wonder	looked, stared

EXTENSIONS

Suggest to students the following:

- type "fairies in fantasy tales" into a search engine to find a range of "fairy stories."
- design posters for current school activities.
- use a poster as a prompt to present a mini-topic on a chosen subject.

FAIRIES IN THE GARDEN

Name _____

Read the fantasy story and answer the questions on the following pages.

The friends lay exhausted on the grass. They had been playing all afternoon in Alice's garden, and now all they wanted to do was watch the wispy clouds float gently across the early-evening sky.

"An elephant squirting water," sighed Robert lazily.

"No, definitely a giraffe with a large . . ."

"Fairies!" squealed Tom as he jumped up and dove behind the bushes next to the shed and slithered through the long grass beyond.

Tom felt as if he was crawling through a tunnel. He struggled a little but soon found he was able to stand up. All around him, a strange glow from tiny lanterns strung between flowers and tree stumps lit up the dark corner of the garden. He was aware of something tickling his bare feet.

As he looked down, he saw bright lights buzzing around his ankles. He was beginning to feel rather strange. He bent down to take a closer look. His eyes opened wide in amazement. Winged fairies of different colors were dancing around a blazing fire.

Suddenly, a beautiful white fairy with delicate, gossamer wings and eyes as bright as sapphires landed on the end of his nose.

"Hello! My name's Morning Glory. Come and join us. We're celebrating Midsummer's Eve."

Tom crouched down and gazed in wonder as the fairies danced and played. Flat pebbles were covered with spider-web tablecloths, and petal plates were filled with grass-seed cookies. To satisfy their thirst, the fairies drank the sweet evening dew that lay heavy on the grass.

After much singing and laughter, the fairies began to tire, and one by one, they curled up in their soft, sweet-scented flower beds. Tom wanted to stay but thought he should get back. Everyone would be wondering where he was.

He wriggled back through the tunnel and the long grass. As he ran excitedly from the shed, he didn't see the branch lying on the path. He tripped and fell.

". . . bottom," giggled Alice. "What do you think, Tom? Does it look like a giraffe?"

FAIRIES IN THE GARDEN

| **Literal** | Find the answers directly in the text. |

1. Complete the following sentence.

The friends had been playing all afternoon _____.

2. List three things Tom saw in the fairies' corner of the garden.

- _____

   _____

- _____

   _____

- _____

   _____

| **Inferential** | Think about what the text says. |

1. Find two phrases in the text that mean Tom was astonished by what he saw.

- _____

   _____

- _____

   _____

2. What do you think had happened to Tom? Explain your answer.

_____

_____

_____

_____

FAIRIES IN THE GARDEN

Applied   Use what you know about the text and your own experience.

1. Images left to your imagination can be seen in many places, such as clouds in the sky. Can you name other places where you have seen images? What images have you imagined? Do other people see the same thing?

_____

_____

_____

_____

_____

_____

_____

_____

_____

_____

2. "Eyes as bright as sapphires" is a simile—a figure of speech comparing two things often using *like* or *as*. Write four similes of your own.

_____

_____

_____

_____

Name _____

FAIRIES IN THE GARDEN

Use the text on page 85 to help you with this page. To complete the table, find each word in the story, and use clues from the text to help you write a definition for each.

Word	Clues	Definition
exhausted		
wispy		
slithered		
amazement		
gossamer		
crouched		
gazed		

Genre: Newspaper Article

READING FOCUS

- Analyzes and extracts information from a newspaper article to answer literal, inferential, and applied questions
- Uses synthesis to plan and write an email based on the information contained in a newspaper article

ANSWER KEY

Literal (Page 91)

1. a panel of educational experts

2. He or she leaves the show.

3. a. Chantal Murray

   b. *Teacher's Pets*

   c. a new car or gold jewelry

   d. Today Television

Inferential (Page 91)

Answers will vary. Possible answer(s): patience, creativity, tenacity, authoritative, energetic, nurturing.

Applied (Page 92)

1–3. Answers will vary.

Applying Strategies (Page 93)

1. a–c. Answers will vary.

2. Answers will vary. The email should include some points from question #1.

EXTENSIONS

- The class can collect articles from newspapers and the Internet. Use them as examples to help the students write their own articles.

- Using the articles collected, students can circle opinions and underline factual statements.

Name _____

Read the newspaper article and answer the questions on the following pages.

If you are an experienced teacher looking for a career challenge, the producers of a new reality television show would love to hear from you.

Teacher's Pets will challenge 12 teachers to teach classes of "tough" students from all over the country. Each teacher will be judged by a panel of educational experts on his or her ability to handle a class.

"The teachers will be asked to teach the children a number of different lessons," said Wayne Jackson, a producer with Today Television. "They will be judged on their ability to teach and how they discipline the children. A score will then be awarded to each teacher."

The teacher with the lowest score from each week will be asked to leave the show. The teacher left at the end of the series will win a collection of prizes, from a new car to gold jewelry.

"The winner will definitely deserve the prizes by the end of the show," said Jackson. "We will be asking some of the children to misbehave as much as possible to give the teachers a hard time. But it should be fun and educational for people of all ages to watch."

However, Superintendent Chantal Murray disagrees with the idea of the show and has asked all teachers to "stay away."

"This show will only give children the incentive to misbehave in class," she said. "It will also discourage potential future teachers from pursuing a career in education. I am disgusted with Today Television and wish they would change their minds about making this show."

But according to Wayne Jackson, it is too late for that. He claims he has already been contacted by thousands of teachers who would like to take up the challenge.

"We are still looking for more people, however," he said. "Teachers can contact us up until the end of this month if they would like the chance to win some fabulous prizes."

TEACHERS ON TV

Literal   Find the answers directly in the text.

1. Who will judge the contestants in the new television show?

_____

2. What happens to the teacher with the lowest score each week?

_____

_____

3. What is:

    a. the superintendent's name?

    _____

    b. the name of the new television show?

    _____

    c. one of the prizes the winner of the show might receive?

    _____

    d. the name of the company Jackson works for?

    _____

Inferential   Think about what the text says.

List four qualities you think a teacher would need to be the winner of the new television show.

-   _____

-   _____

-   _____

-   _____

TEACHERS ON TV

Applied   Use what you know about the text and your own experience.

1. Do you agree with the superintendent's point of view?   ☐ Yes ☐ No

   Explain your answer. _____

   _____

   _____

2. Which group of people do you think the new television show would be most popular with?

   ☐ children   ☐ teenagers   ☐ teachers   ☐ parents   ☐ grandparents

   Write reasons for your answer.

   _____

   _____

   _____

3. What could be another premise for a show about teachers that would have a more positive response? What would the challenge be for the teachers?

   _____

   _____

   _____

   _____

   _____

   _____

   _____

   _____

   _____

TEACHERS ON TV

Use the text on page 90 to help you complete this page. Imagine you are a teacher. You decide to email Wayne Jackson to show your interest in being a contestant and ask some questions about the show.

1. Plan your email in the space below.

    a. List three reasons why you are interested in being on the show.

        • _____

        • _____

        • _____

    b. List three qualities that would make you a good contestant.

        • _____

        • _____

        • _____

    c. Write three questions you have about the show.

        • _____

        • _____

        • _____

2. Use some of the ideas that are in your plan to write your email.

_____

_____

_____

_____

_____

_____

_____

Genre: Fairy Tale

READING FOCUS

- Analyzes and extracts information from a fairy tale to answer literal, inferential, and applied questions
- Summarizes the setting, characters, main events, and themes contained in a fairy tale
- Compares the main elements of two fairy tales

ANSWER KEY

Literal (Page 96)

1. The three drawings should be of a field, a pear tree, and a well.

2. a. 2   b. 3   c. 1   d. 4

Inferential (Page 96)

1–2. Answers will vary.

Applied (Page 97)

1–2. Answers will vary.

Applying Strategies (Page 98)

1. **Setting**—in the forest and the palace, in a faraway land
   Characters—wicked magician, the king, queen, Princess Safia, courtiers, the mouse (the Prince), Wise Woman, green ogre
   Important Events—
   The princess asked the mouse for help, so the mouse took her to see the Wise Woman.
   The Wise Woman told her to take the pear on the highest branch from a pear tree and feed it to the green ogre in the well.
   The mouse turned back into a prince once the spell was broken.
   The magician shrank the royal family and hid them in a cupboard. He became king until Princess Safia put him into a deep sleep, and all his spells were broken.
   Ideas—Answers will vary.

2. Answers will vary.

EXTENSIONS

- Students can read other fairy tales and fractured fairy tales, such as:
  - *Snow White in New York* by Fiona French
  - *Princess Smartypants* by Babette Cole
  - *The Paperbag Princess* by Robert Munsch
  - *Revolting Rhymes* by Roald Dahl
  - *Legally Correct Fairy Tales* by David Fisher
- A variety of fairy tales from other countries can be found on the Internet by typing "fairy tale" and the name of the country into a search engine.

THE PRINCESS AND THE MOUSE

Name _____

Read the Arabian fairy tale and answer the questions on the following pages.

Once upon a time, in a faraway land, there lived a wicked magician who wanted to be king. So he disguised himself as a wise professor and asked the king if he could have a room at the palace to work in. The king agreed.

Soon after, the magician captured the king and queen's only child, Princess Safia. He cast a spell on her until she shrank to the size of his thumb and then put her in a cupboard that was in his room. He then captured the king and the queen, shrank both of them, and also put them in a cupboard.

The news of the royal family's disappearance soon spread around the palace. The courtiers came to the magician.

"Wise professor, please tell us what to do!" they cried.

"Make me the ruler of this land until the king is found," said the magician. The courtiers agreed, and the magician took the throne. He sent out troops to look for the royal family, knowing they would never be found.

Some time passed. One night, a mouse gnawed a hole in the magician's cupboard and was astonished to see the tiny princess. She pleaded for help. The mouse took her to see the Wise Woman, who lived in a hollow tree in the forest.

The Wise Woman told Princess Safia that she would need to go on a journey to make things right again. "Go to the nearest field," she said. "The horse you will find there will take you to a pear tree. Pick the pear on the highest branch. The pear is the magician's soul. The horse will then take you to the well of the green ogre, who lives at the bottom of the well. Drop the pear into his mouth, and he will eat it. The magician will fall into a deep sleep instantly. When he does, everything he has cast a spell on will return to normal."

Princess Safia did as the Wise Woman said. As soon as the ogre ate the pear, she returned to her normal size again. She rode back to the palace to find the magician, who was lying peacefully, and her parents, who had also returned to their normal size. The princess told them what had happened.

While the whole palace rejoiced, Princess Safia went back to the forest to thank the Wise Woman. But instead, she found a handsome prince.

"The Wise Woman has gone," he said.

"Who are you?" asked Princess Safia.

"I was the mouse," said the Prince. "I, too, had a spell cast on me by the wicked magician."

Princess Safia and the prince fell in love and were soon married. They lived happily ever after.

THE PRINCESS AND THE MOUSE

Literal   Find the answers directly in the text.

1. Draw and label the three locations the Wise Woman told the princess to go to.

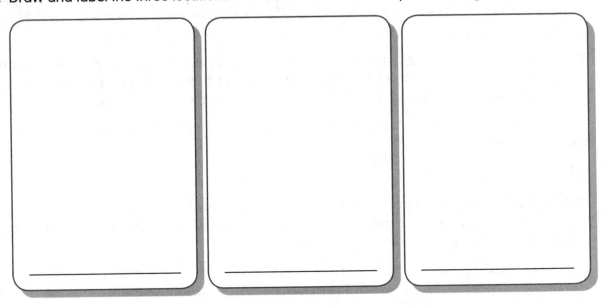

_____   _____   _____

2. Number these events from 1–4 in the order in which they happened in the text.

a. _____ The wicked magician took the throne.

b. _____ The ogre ate the pear.

c. _____ The king and queen shrank.

d. _____ Princess Safia saw the handsome prince.

Inferential   Think about what the text says.

1. Why do you think the magician fell into a deep sleep when the ogre ate the pear?

_____

_____

2. Do you think the magician was clever?   ☐ Yes ☐ No

Explain your answer. _____

_____

THE PRINCESS AND THE MOUSE

Applied   Use what you know about the text and your own experience.

1. Imagine that Safia decided to ignore the Wise Woman's advice. Instead, she wrote a plan for how to get her father back on the throne. Write the steps you think her plan might have contained.

_____

_____

_____

_____

_____

_____

_____

2. The Wise Woman told Princess Safia to go on this particular journey to make things right again. Imagine you were the Wise Woman, and have Princess Safia take a different journey that would make things right.

_____

_____

_____

_____

_____

_____

_____

_____

THE PRINCESS AND THE MOUSE

Use the fairy tale from page 95 to complete the following activities.

1. Summarize "The Princess and the Mouse" on page 95 by completing the table.

Setting	Characters
Important Events	
The princess _____ _____ _____	**Ideas**
	Wicked people should _____ _____ _____.
The Wise Woman _____ _____ _____	Princesses should _____
	_____
The mouse _____ _____ _____	_____ _____.
The magician _____ _____ _____	Magic can be used to _____ _____ _____.

2. Many fairy tales have similar settings, characters, events, and ideas. Think about a fairy tale you know to complete the sentences below.

Comparing

I think "The Princess and the Mouse" is similar to this fairy tale: _____

_____

This is because _____

_____

_____

Genre: Adventure

READING FOCUS

- Analyzes and extracts information from an adventure narrative to answer literal, inferential, and applied questions

- Summarizes the events in a narrative from a character's point of view

- Makes connections between the decisions made by the characters in a narrative and his/her own decisions

ANSWER KEY

Literal (Page 101)

1. "Try our ghost train adventure—if you dare!"

2. a. False   b. True   c. False   d. True

Inferential (Page 101)

1. The ghost train was old—the text mentioned the flaking paint inside the carriage.

2. Answers will vary. Possible answer(s): startled, surprised, worried, angry, panicked.

3. Answers will vary. Possible answer(s): no one would think to look for stolen money in an amusement park ride; it wasn't a popular ride.

Applied (Page 102)

Answers will vary.

Applying Strategies (Page 103)

1. Answers will vary.

2. a–b. Answers will vary.

EXTENSIONS

- Students can read other adventure stories, such as:
  - *Redwall* series by Brian Jacques
  - *The Chronicles of Narnia* by C.S. Lewis
  - *A Series of Unfortunate Events* by Lemony Snicket

Name _____

Read the adventure story and answer the questions on the following pages.

TRY OUR GHOST TRAIN ADVENTURE—IF YOU DARE!

Jenna read the sign one last time and settled herself in the small carriage. She and Hayden were the only passengers, which wasn't surprising. The ride didn't look scary at all.

"When's this boring thing going to start?" her brother said, picking at the flaking paint inside the carriage.

As he spoke, the train shuddered and rattled into the dim tunnel. A skeleton lowered itself slowly from the ceiling. Jenna sighed.

"That's so fake. It . . ."

She suddenly jolted in the seat. The train had come to a halt.

"Oh, no," said Hayden. "It's broken down! What are we going to do?"

"Well, I'm not going to hang around here waiting," said Jenna. "Let's get out and walk the rest of it." She and Hayden clambered out of the carriage and started along the track. But after a few steps, they had to stop. The track had split into two. One track went uphill, the other down.

"Which way do . . . ?" Hayden began. Then he paused. "I can hear voices."

"What?" Jenna listened carefully. Hayden was right. There were at least two people talking. The sound was coming from the direction of the downhill track.

"We'll wait until the ride's finished, then we'll hide the money," one voice said. "No one would think to look here."

"I can't hear the train," said another voice. "It must have moved past us. Let's carry it up now."

Jenna looked at Hayden. "Quick, let's hide." She darted behind a large, plastic-looking rock. Hayden scooted in next to her. They then both peered over it. Two men, dressed in dark clothing, were making their way toward them. One was carrying a large bag. Jenna's eyes widened. She had seen both men on TV last night. They were the main suspects in a bank robbery.

Hayden gasped loudly. One of the men paused and snapped his head in Jenna and Hayden's direction. "What was . . . Hey, there's some kids there! Look!"

Hayden grabbed Jenna's hand and pulled her to her feet. "Come on!"

Jenna stumbled out from behind the rock and ended up just in front of the men. She twisted out of their grasping hands and fled up the track after Hayden. She hoped he'd chosen the best way. Maybe the sign had been right. This ride was turning out to be an adventure after all.

GHOST TRAIN ADVENTURE

Literal   Find the answers directly in the text.

1. What was written on the sign Jenna was reading?

_____

_____

2. Read each sentence. Decide if each statement is **True** or **False**.

    a. The train stopped before Jenna saw
    the skeleton.   ☐ True ☐ False

    b. Hayden gasped when he saw the men.   ☐ True ☐ False

    c. Jenna wanted to wait in the train.   ☐ True ☐ False

    d. Hayden and Jenna hid behind a large
    plastic rock.   ☐ True ☐ False

Inferential   Think about what the text says.

1. Was the ghost train most likely old or new? Give a reason for your answer.

_____

_____

2. Write words to describe how you think the men might have felt when they realized Hayden and Jenna were watching them.

_____

_____

3. Why do you think the men might have chosen the ghost train ride as a place to hide their money? Write two possibilities.

    • _____

    • _____

GHOST TRAIN ADVENTURE

Applied   Use what you know about the text and your own experience.

Continue the adventure and write an ending for the story. What happens to Jenna and Hayden? What happens to the robbers?

_____

_____

_____

_____

_____

_____

_____

_____

_____

_____

_____

_____

_____

_____

_____

_____

_____

_____

_____

_____

GHOST TRAIN ADVENTURE

Summarizing

Use the text on page 100 to help you complete this page.

1. We see the events in this story through Jenna's eyes. How do you think Hayden might describe what happened? Write a summary from his point of view, as if he is telling a friend what took place.

   _____

   _____

   _____

   _____

2. Jenna and Hayden had to make many decisions during the story. Consider two of their decisions below. Think about whether you would have done the same, and explain why or why not.

   Making Connections

   a. Would you have left the train as soon as it stopped?　☐ Yes　☐ No

   If not, what would you have done instead? _____

   _____

   Explain your decision. _____

   _____

   _____

   b. Would you have followed the uphill track?　☐ Yes　☐ No

   If not, what would you have done instead? _____

   _____

   Explain your decision. _____

   _____

   _____

Genre: Poetry—a legend written in poetic form

READING FOCUS

- Analyzes and extracts information from a poem to answer literal, inferential, and applied questions
- Scans information in a poem

ANSWER KEY

Literal (Page 106)

Main Characters	Hina, Maui, the Sun
Setting for the Poem	a tropical land
Main Events or Action	Answers will vary but should be similar to the following: Hina works really hard making cloth. Maui, her son, wants to make things easier for her by trying to get the Sun to slow down his movements so that she has time to dry her cloth. He captures the Sun with ropes and won't let him go until he agrees to move slowly through the sky at certain times of the year. The Sun agrees. Maui lets him go, and the Sun keeps his bargain so that Hina has plenty of time to dry her cloth.

Inferential (Page 106)

1. a. hardworking, weary, strong   b. angry, likes to fight, impatient, cunning

   c. punctual, fast, agreeable, strong, reliable

2. travels; longer

Applied (Page 107)

Answers will vary.

Applying Strategies (Page 108)

1. a. mad/tired   b. falls/call   c. threads/end   d. near/snare

2. a. Eight of the following adjectives: tropical (land); afternoon (fog); aching, tired (Hina); too short (the day); damp (the cloth); strong (cords); sleeping (Sun); tight (the noose); bright, warm, clear (the sky); happy (Maui)

   b. Eight of the following verbs: gathered, soaked, pounded, paddled, waited, slipped, tied, cried, dried

3. Answers will vary.

EXTENSIONS

- Students can write well-known legends in their own words or attempt to write them in poetic form.
- The teacher can read a small section of an epic poem, such as *The Odyssey*, to the students.
- Students can conduct research to find other myths or legends written in poetic form.

Name _____

Read the legend written in poetic form and answer the questions on the following pages.

A long time ago in a tropical land,
Hina, the goddess, made cloth by hand.
She gathered the bark from the mulberry trees,
Then soaked it in water gathered from the seas.
She pounded it flat on a kapa log,
Then left it to dry in the afternoon fog.
Maui, her son, would get quite mad
To see her working—always aching and tired.
"The day is too short," she would often say.
"The sun goes away before I finish for the day.
The cloth is still damp when nightime falls,
So it stays that way till dawn starts to call."
"The Sun is to blame," said Maui with a frown.
"He travels too fast and needs to slow down."
Maui wove some snares from coconut threads
Into eight strong cords with a noose on each end.
He paddled to the land of the sleeping Sun,
Set his snares and waited for the fun.
The Sun awoke as dawn came near.
Each ray of the Sun slipped into Maui's snare.
Maui drew each noose up tight,
Then tied them to rocks to stop the Sun's flight.
"What have you done?" the Sun cried out,
"Your world will die if you don't let me out!"
"Listen to my plan, and if you agree,
I'll undo the snares and set you free.
You will travel slowly for part of the year.
The sky will be bright and warm and clear."
The Sun gave his word and was soon on his way.
The pattern of life was set from that day.
Hina dried her cloth in the warmth from the Sun.
Maui was happy because of what he had done.

Name _____

HINA, MAUI, AND THE CAPTURED SUN

| **Literal** | Find the answers directly in the text. |

Complete the table below.

Main Characters	
Setting for the Poem	
Main Events or Action	

| **Inferential** | Think about what the text says. |

1. Place an **X** in the boxes next to the words or phrases that describe the main characters.

a. Hina   ☐ hardworking   ☐ lazy   ☐ impatient

  ☐ strong   ☐ weary   ☐ young

b. Maui   ☐ calm   ☐ angry   ☐ old   ☐ likes to fight

  ☐ impatient   ☐ kind   ☐ nasty   ☐ cunning

c. Sun   ☐ punctual   ☐ fast   ☐ stubborn   ☐ agreeable

  ☐ strong   ☐ arrogant   ☐ reliable

2. Complete the following sentence.

For part of the year, the Sun _____ slowly, so the days are _____.

HINA, MAUI, AND THE CAPTURED SUN

Applied   Use what you know about the text and your own experience.

Maui was a young demigod who used a cunning plan to get what he wanted from a stronger god—the Sun. Write a similar story in which a similar thing happens.

_____

_____

_____

_____

_____

_____

_____

_____

_____

_____

_____

_____

_____

_____

_____

_____

_____

_____

_____

_____

_____

HINA, MAUI, AND THE CAPTURED SUN

Use the legend written in poetic form from page 105 to complete the following activites. This poem uses mostly rhyming couplets (a set of two lines, in which the last word in each line rhymes with the other). For example, *land/hand*; *trees/seas*.

1. In the space below, write the last words of each set of two lines that do not fit the rhyming pattern.

   a. _____ and _____

   b. _____ and _____

   c. _____ and _____

   d. _____ and _____

2. **a.** Write eight adjectives used in the poem that describe a character, place, or thing.

   _____   _____

   _____   _____

   _____   _____

   _____   _____

   b. Write eight verbs from the poem ending in -*ed*.

   _____   _____

   _____   _____

   _____   _____

3. Why do you think the poet used direct speech (the actual words the characters said) in the poem? Were they used effectively? Explain your answer.

   _____

   _____

   _____

Common Core State Standards

Standards Correlations

Each lesson meets one or more of the following Common Core State Standards © Copyright 2010. National Governors Association Center for Best Practices and Council of Chief State School Officers. All rights reserved. For more information about the Common Core State Standards, go to *http://www.corestandards.org/* or *http://www.teachercreated.com/standards*.

Reading Literature/Fiction Text Standards	Text Title	Pages
Key Ideas and Details		
ELA.RL.4.1 Refer to details and examples in a text when explaining what the text says explicitly and when drawing inferences from the text.	The Clever Judge	9–13
	Three Fables	19–23
	Back to Sivrax?	29–33
	Little John	44–48
	Lost!	49–53
	Mystery in the Night	54–58
	The New Girl	59–63
	The Story of Gelert	64–68
	Fairies in the Garden	84–88
	The Princess and the Mouse	94–98
	Ghost Train Adventure	99–103
	Hina, Maui, and the Captured Sun	104–108
ELA.RL.4.2 Determine a theme of a story, drama, or poem from details in the text; summarize the text.	The Clever Judge	9–13
	Three Fables	19–23
	Little John	44–48
	Lost!	49–53
	Mystery in the Night	54–58
	The New Girl	59–63
	The Story of Gelert	64–68
	Fairies in the Garden	84–88
	The Princess and the Mouse	94–98
	Ghost Train Adventure	99–103
	Hina, Maui, and the Captured Sun	104–108
ELA.RL.4.3 Describe in depth a character, setting, or event in a story or drama, drawing on specific details in the text (e.g., a character's thoughts, words, or actions).	The Clever Judge	9–13
	Three Fables	19–23
	Back to Sivrax?	29–33
	Little John	44–48
	Lost!	49–53
	Mystery in the Night	54–58
	The New Girl	59–63
	The Princess and the Mouse	94–98

Reading Literature/Fiction Text Standards *(cont.)*	Text Title	Pages
Craft and Structure		
ELA.RL.4.4 Determine the meaning of words and phrases as they are used in a text, including those that allude to significant characters found in mythology (e.g., Herculean).	The Clever Judge Little John Mystery in the Night The Story of Gelert Fairies in the Garden Ghost Train Adventure Hina, Maui, and the Captured Sun	9–13 44–48 54–58 64–68 84–88 99–103 104–108
ELA.RL.4.5 Explain major differences between poems, drama, and prose, and refer to the structural elements of poems (e.g., verse, rhythm, meter) and drama (e.g., casts of characters, settings, descriptions, dialogue, stage directions) when writing or speaking about a text.	Little John Hina, Maui, and the Captured Sun	44–48 104–108
ELA.RL.4.6 Compare and contrast the point of view from which different stories are narrated, including the difference between first- and third-person narrations.	Ghost Train Adventure	99–103
Integration of Knowledge and Ideas		
ELA.RL.4.7 Make connections between the text of a story or drama and a visual or oral presentation of the text, identifying where each version reflects specific descriptions and directions in the text.	Little John	44–48
ELA.RL.4.9 Compare and contrast the treatment of similar themes and topics (e.g., opposition of good and evil) and patterns of events (e.g., the quest) in stories, myths, and traditional literature from different cultures.	The Princess and the Mouse	94–98
Range of Reading and Level of Text Complexity		
ELA.RL.4.10 By the end of the year, read and comprehend literature, including stories, dramas, and poetry, in the grades 4–5 text complexity band proficiently, with scaffolding as needed at the high end of the range.	The Clever Judge Three Fables Back to Sivrax? Little John Lost! Mystery in the Night The New Girl The Story of Gelert Fairies in the Garden The Princess and the Mouse Ghost Train Adventure Hina, Maui, and the Captured Sun	9–13 19–23 29–33 44–48 49–53 54–58 59–63 64–68 84–88 94–98 99–103 104–108

Common Core State Standards (cont.)

Reading Informational Text/Nonfiction Standards	Text Title	Pages
Key Ideas and Details		
ELA.RI.4.1 Refer to details and examples in a text when explaining what the text says explicitly and when drawing inferences from the text.	What's On? Scones Enid Blyton A Threat to Polar Bears The Journal of Kublai Khan Letters for a Purpose Concert "All-Round Disappointment" Teachers on TV	14–18 24–28 34–38 39–43 69–73 74–78 79–83 89–93
ELA.RI.4.2 Determine the main idea of a text and explain how it is supported by key details; summarize the text.	What's On? A Threat to Polar Bears The Journal of Kublai Khan Letters for a Purpose Concert "All-Round Disappointment" Teachers on TV	14–18 39–43 69–73 74–78 79–83 89–93
ELA.RI.4.3 Explain events, procedures, ideas, or concepts in a historical, scientific, or technical text, including what happened and why, based on specific information in the text.	What's On? Scones A Threat to Polar Bears The Journal of Kublai Khan	14–18 24–28 39–43 69–73
Craft and Structure		
ELA.RI.4.4 Determine the meaning of general academic and domain-specific words or phrases in a text relevant to a *grade 4 topic or subject area*.	What's On? Scones A Threat to Polar Bears The Journal of Kublai Khan	14–18 24–28 39–43 69–73
ELA.RI.4.5 Describe the overall structure (e.g., chronology, comparison, cause/effect, problem/solution) of events, ideas, concepts, or information in a text or part of a text.	What's On? Enid Blyton A Threat to Polar Bears The Journal of Kublai Khan Letters for a Purpose Concert "All-Round Disappointment"	14–18 34–38 39–43 69–73 74–78 79–83

Reading Informational Text/Nonfiction Standards *(cont.)*	Text Title	Pages
Integration of Knowledge and Ideas		
ELA.RI.4.7 Interpret information presented visually, orally, or quantitatively (e.g., in charts, graphs, diagrams, time lines, animations, or interactive elements on Web pages) and explain how the information contributes to an understanding of the text in which it appears.	What's On? Scones Enid Blyton A Threat to Polar Bears	14–18 24–28 34–38 39–43
ELA.RI.4.8 Explain how an author uses reasons and evidence to support particular points in a text.	A Threat to Polar Bears The Journal of Kublai Khan Concert "All-Round Disappointment" Teachers on TV	39–43 69–73 79–83 89–93
Range of Reading and Level of Text Complexity		
ELA.RI.4.10 By the end of year, read and comprehend informational texts, including history/social studies, science, and technical texts, in the grades 4–5 text complexity band proficiently, with scaffolding as needed at the high end of the range.	What's On? Scones Enid Blyton A Threat to Polar Bears The Journal of Kublai Khan Letters for a Purpose Concert "All-Round Disappointment" Teachers on TV	14–18 24–28 34–38 39–43 69–73 74–78 79–83 89–93